Please return to WA Rosenbaum

The FAT
Is in Your Head

A LIFE STYLE TO KEEP IT OFF

THE FAT IS IN YOUR HEAD

Charlie W. Shedd

WORD BOOKS, Publisher
Waco, Texas

Quotations from the Revised Standard Version of the Bible, copyright 1946 and 1952 by the Division of Christian Education of the National Council of Churches of Christ in the United States of America, used by permission; the Today's English Version of the New Testament, copyright © American Bible Society, 1966; *The New English Bible* © The Delegates of The Oxford University Press and The Syndics of The Cambridge University Press, 1961, 1970, reprinted by permission; *The New Testament in Modern English* by J. B. Phillips, © J. B. Phillips 1958; *A New Translation of the Bible* by James Moffatt, copyright, 1922, 1924, 1926, 1935, by Harper & Brothers, *The Living Bible* © 1962, 1965, 1966, 1967, 1968, 1970, 1971 by Tyndale House Publishers, Wheaton, Illinois; *The New Testament in Basic English*, Cambridge University Press in association with Evans Bros. Ltd.; *The New Testament in Modern Speech* by Richard Francis Weymouth, copyright 1943, 1944 by The Pilgrim Press; *The New Testament: An American Translation* by Edgar J. Goodspeed, copyright © 1923, 1948 by the University of Chicago; *The Epistles of Paul* by W. J. Conybeare, Baker Book House; *The New Testament in Modern English* translated by Helen Barrett Montgomery, copyright © 1924, 1952 by the American Baptist Board of Education and Publication, The Judson Press. All Scripture quotations are identified in the text by name of translator or abbreviations in conventional form.

ISBN 0-87680 202-1

Library of Congress catalog card number: 72-76443
Printed in the United States of America

To you, my fellow fatty.

You've been looking for answers a long time. I know because I've been there with you. And I found my answer in a psychospiritual approach.

Most of us heavies know that pounds are not our only problem. Something is bugging us besides our avoirdupois. What goes in our minds can be every bit as important as what we eat.

Yet even a full knowledge of our kinky selves is not enough. Analysis won't do it alone. We need synthesis. That's why the spiritual must go hand in hand with the psychological.

So, if you believe God made you,
  if you even slightly suspect you're not
    shaping up to his pattern,
      if you're willing to elect a new chairman
        of the board way down in your soul,
          this book is dedicated to you.

Contents

Acknowledgments

Throughout this book, the author emphasizes the importance of medical advice for all reducing efforts. We're grateful to the following doctors who read this manuscript prior to publication and gave valuable suggestions:

Donald S. Kellam, M.D., Orthopedic Surgeon, Charlotte, North Carolina

James Mallory, M.D., Psychiatrist, Atlanta, Georgia

Max Mertz, Ph.D., Psychologist, Houston, Texas

Woodrow W. Payne, M.D., F.A.C.S., Urologist, Brunswick, Georgia

James Pierce, M.D., Industrial Medicine, Indianapolis, Indiana

Bill Williams, M.D., Nashville, Georgia

Plan

This book is not meant to be read in one sitting. Which, if you are like I am, will prompt you to read it in one sitting.

But I put it in forty meditations for day by day study. The report is that Jesus fasted forty days and "afterward he hungered." Sounds reasonable. I famish in a few hours. And I need all the help I can get. For some of us the helpful stuff digests slowly, forty days, forty years, forever. Very few of us have said good-by to the problem permanently.

Medical authorities point to this desolate truth: Most reduction is of brief duration. Few have what it takes to sustain loss for any appreciable period. So the telling question is not *how much* but *how long*.

We must develop a life style to keep it off.

I

I Resign

Homer is one of my favorite people and a big man on prayer. But there are some very unconventional goings on between him and his Maker. I admire him partially because he has fought one of life's toughest problems and come out on top. He tells me his recovery began the day he wrote this two-word letter:

Dear God,
I resign.
Homer

1
To Move a Mountain

". . . *if you have faith as a grain of mustard seed, you will say to this mountain, 'Move hence to yonder place,' and it will move*" (Matt. 17:20, RSV).

Are you one of the overweight millions living life in quiet desperation?

Then you've got company.

Medics tell us too many pounds is the nation's number one health problem. By their statistics more than one hundred million Americans weigh too much. That's half the population. And thirty million of these, they say, are obese. Where we are in this picture depends on whose figures we accept. But after putting them all together, it averages out like this: If we carry 10 percent more than we should, we're overweight; 20 percent classifies us obese.

Yet this one fact stands: What's coming off the exterior isn't as important as what's going on inside.

Fifteen years and one hundred twenty pounds ago, I dropped to my knees and prayed:

Lord, I've tried for years to whip this problem of obesity. I've been on banana diets and eaten red meat. I've taken pills and bought reducing belts. I've read books, attended lectures, joined clubs, enrolled in courses.

But I'm still fat. I weigh much too much. And I need help.

In the Good Book you promise if anyone has enough faith he can say to a mountain, "Go away," and it will go. There's a mountain of flesh on me. I've been trying to move it ever since I was a boy. I've been laughed at. I've been ridiculed. I've rationalized; I've lied. I've had times when I cared and times when I didn't.

I've decided to quit and promised I'd be good. Then we were invited out, and this woman makes the best biscuits. I've sworn off, and before I knew it, I found myself sitting at the fountain lapping a milk shake.

Now I mean business. I accept you at your word. Today I say to this mountain, "Get moving." I have faith that the two of us can move it together. This is the big surrender. I'm turning my body over to you once and for all. I can't manage it alone. From this day on, I'll eat what you tell me to eat and live how you want me to live. *Amen.*

I don't hear voices like some of my friends, but I get the message. And this time the message was: You've come to the right place, the prayer of commitment. This is the prayer where we surrender the chisel. Now we quit carving away at our wants. We turn the tools over to God to shape us his way.

There may be a few for whom the problem is purely physical, but not for most of us. For us the fat is in our head and the cure is in our soul.

2
The Turn to the Mirror

"Thou art waxen fat, thou art grown thick, thou art covered with fatness" (Deut. 32:15).

If we take it personally, this Old Testament writer wasn't being very nice. Some scholars say he was leveling his charge at nations. But like so many other things from the Bible, the verse has individual application.

If we have the courage, these words from Deuteronomy can teach us. They can turn us around and face us down the hall toward the mirror.

It isn't enough to admit we're fat. We must accept it. *Admitting* means tipping the hat in the general direction of our problem. *Acceptance* calls for inner resignation to this truth: We are not what we were meant to be.

Another unusual Homer prayer is what he calls his original-me thing: *Lord, show me what you had in mind when you made me and how you want me now.*

When I first heard this prayer, it cut through me—through all those layers it carved its way to the cause and the cure.

15

Anyone daring to pray Homer's prayer honestly will get the picture. There is often considerable difference between the original and what we have become. Such acceptance is the first step in recovery.

There are several reasons why this prayer is especially effective for the fat person. For one thing, lying and self-deception have a long history with us. We suffer from a murky self-image. And our original is lost in the shadows.

Homer's prayer when it is honestly prayed sweeps away half-truths.

There's a second reason why this prayer can be a big help. Most of us heavies desperately need a new self-image. We live under a derogatory barrage of public opinion. Sure, people aren't smirking as much as we think. Most of them are fully occupied with their own concerns. But still, society, the magazines, the media all point their finger in our direction. Before we know it, we begin to think of ourselves as some kind of special freak. Yet even this is not as bad as our low-grade self-disdain. Frequent failure and constant self-incrimination weigh almost as heavy as our pounds.

Homer's prayer for a new self-image brings with it a third plus. It purifies our motives. Most fat people know how easy it is to live for false reasons.

There is nothing wrong with wanting to lose so we will look better. In our clothes. On the beach. Before other people. At the mirror.

Nothing wrong either with wanting to live longer, work better, move with more grace, think faster.

But genuine prayer purges our motives. It takes us from good reasons to the best. And the best for us is like the man said, "Lord, show me what you had in mind when you made me and how you want me now."

"Watch and pray"
(Matt. 26:41; Mark 14:38).

3
Constant Ambush

From the year 1850 comes this warning, "The hourly watch over the instinctive desires, which must be observed by one desirous of reducing his corpulence, make it a solemn thing. He that commences it must be taught to view himself as his worst enemy; like the philosopher in Epictetus, he must 'mount guard, and lie in constant ambush against himself.' " [1]

We know what you mean, friend. Our kind of self-supervision is a solemn thing. And we don't like it. For years we have taken the easy way. This is our habit and it dies hard.

We have done a big thing for ourselves when we accept this fact: On our way to heaven, we may feel like hell.

For one thing we are too easily taken by the admakers' lie: Feel great, lose weight.

That is never how it is. We may feel better *after* we have lost. But while we are losing, we may feel awful.

---

1. T. K. Chamber, *Corpulence: On Excess of Fat in the Human Body* (London: Longman and Co., 1850).

There is a whimsical saying which shows up often in writings on the psychology of obesity. This has the feel of the real: "When a woman goes on a diet, it's not her bones, but her nerves which stick out first."

Because that's how it is, nobody ever gets holy enough to dismiss the inner sentries. But we were never promised high country all the time. Jesus had his struggles, and we will. In both Matthew and Mark, he tells us to "*watch and pray*."

The word *watch* which he uses here means to be vigilant, to pay attention.

Some people eat in their sleep. These, say the psychiatrists, are the most serious cases. But some of us shade off this problem with a tricky version of our own.

For me the last six waking hours of every day are hunger time. Sure, I know, "Eat early to prevent late hunger." "Don't skip meals." "Breakfast is especially important." So I've gone those routes, but they all dead end at the same place. No matter what I do, toward late afternoon my old nemesis begins to bear down. Subconsciously my watcher nods.

I've psyched out every imaginable angle. Am I coming home famished from school again? Is my mother's well-filled cookie jar luring me? Could it be the cozy-up-to-each-other-as-darkness-comes-on thing? Far down inside am I trying to recapture sensations tucked away in my past?

To which comes the monotonous answer—some things are lost forever in my history. With these I must face facts, quit fussing, build walls against the enemy. For me, this means a few moments of quiet before meals whenever possible. It means prayer—by myself or with someone who loves me. It means midafternoon rededication, and recommitment as the sun goes down.

QUESTION: Will we ever be so sure of ourselves that we can dismiss our constant watchers?

ANSWER: Probably not. Though we stun the ravenous self temporarily, to paralyze him permanently seems next to impossible. Our friend of 1850 is right. For long-term results, we must mount guard and lie in constant ambush against ourselves.

4
One Handful of Peanuts

"Set a watch, O Lord, before my mouth; keep the door of my lips" (Ps. 141:3, 4).

One handful of peanuts is all it takes to do us in.

Others may be able to eat with moderation. But not us. We are the compulsives. That's what the psychiatrists call us. Which being interpreted, means we might go berserk with a single bite.

POINT TO REMEMBER: That first mouthful is all important. This word of the psalmist is more than an admonition to watch what we say. It's a good prayer also for guarding our intake before meals, dessert, snack time . . . before the guests arrive or we're invited out . . . before vacations, picnics, bedtime . . . before Thanksgiving . . . before Christmas . . . before any festive occasion . . . before potluck dinners. At these things I've even caught myself eating stuff I didn't want. God only knows what sins have been sinned by fat Christians at church dinners.[1]

---

1. Is overeating sin? Some experts thrash around a long time for proper terminology. Should we call our problem sickness, disease, weakness, or miscellaneous variants? I have no special enlightenment on the harangue for correct labels. By any other name, it's my fat. Yet our catechism says, "Sin is any transgression of the law of God." If I know I shouldn't eat something and I do it anyway, what else can I call it?

Abstinence is the key word for the alcoholic. Until he makes friends with this, he can't quit drinking. But if he has what it takes, he solves his problem when he stops altogether.

For us it's tougher. We have to eat *something*. Three times a day we must answer the question: Will we or won't we eat with control?

Then, even if we win at mealtime, there are still our favorites. They jump up and down. They clamor for attention. Damnable. Ever present: Ice cream . . . chocolates . . . pecan pie . . . peanut brittle . . . popcorn . . . nuts on the table . . . mints in the jar . . . cake in the box.

And as though this were not enough, our frenzy changes with the passing seasons. Corn on the cob . . . dressing and gravy . . . banana nut bread . . . Dutch apple strudel.

Every chubby daughter of Eve has stood by the bakery window and fought these gastronomical lures. Every weighty son of Adam has experienced an inner war with the desserts listed so innocently on the menu.

STRATEGIC QUESTION: Will this really feed my deepest hunger? Although it looks like the finest fare, would an inner renunciation right now give me more lasting satisfaction?

✿ ✿ ✿ ✿ ✿ ✿ ✿

We must go to our meals in the spirit of holy simplicity paying more attention to God than to what we are eating.[2]

---

2. John Nicholas Grou (1731–1803), *Manual for Interior Souls* (London: The Broadwater Press, Ltd.), p. 270.

If one aims at a fundamental cure,
there is no other way to recovery than
the way that leads through
despair. Much as one would like
to lead the patient gently over the hill
. . . this is usually not possible.[1]

5

Fighting Those Get-Me-Down Blues

"My soul is weary of my life" (Job 10:1).

Nomination for life's darkest day: When I have been faithful to my diet and lost zero. We know what you mean, Job. Sometimes serving the Lord is a drag. Those get-me-down blues make another chapter from our life. At times the going is low, low, lower and it's dark down here.

Research among psychiatric writers turns up numerous reports from these low regions. Here is a typical observation on the study of eighteen patients referred to a psychiatrist.

> The most frequently expressed emotional stimulus to eating was feeling blue, discouraged, or depressed. Patients stated they ate more than usual when tense or upset. They said when nervous, anxious, lonely, bored, a snack would in some way make them feel better.[2]

1. Andras Angyal, *Neurosis and Treatment* (New York: John Wiley & Sons, Inc., 1965), p. 225.
2. W. W. Hamburger, "Psychological Aspects of Obesity," *Bulletin N.Y. Academy Medicine*, November 1957, p. 776.

WARNING: Whenever we begin eating our heart out, it's time to be extra careful. We may be eating our stomach full to get back on the sunny side! Yet it is precisely at this moment that we might be poised at the winner's circle.

Whether these blue-mood binges are physiological, psychological, or spiritual nobody seems to know. But I think it works like this. Inside, sometimes the tough hangers-on are waiting to be convinced. And their hammerlock can only be broken if I stubbornly refuse to give up. Is this simply a matter of glands and genes or other mysterious things? Could it be the Inner Presence waiting to see whether I really mean my commitment?

The daughter of one of our friends was first runner-up in a national beauty contest. "Anyway you look at it," her father said, "that has to be bottom spot. Nothing could ever hurt more than almost but not quite."

Some may argue his premise. But there is no question about this: To give up on the verge of victory makes double blue.

Job's biographer concludes on the note: "And the Lord blessed the latter days of Job more than his beginning."

That's still how it is today. With some things, God's blessings are reserved for those who stay right in there.

✿ ✿ ✿ ✿ ✿ ✿ ✿

PRAYER: Lord, when my soul is weary of my life, help me to tough it through. I may not like these days, but I do like you. I want to be loyal to your call. *Amen.*

"Delays occur in order to test your fidelity." [3]

3. Thomas Fry, Jr., *Doing What Comes Supernaturally* (Old Tappan, N.J.: Fleming H. Revell, 1966), p. 96.

Adversity with his pick
mines the heart, but he is a cunning
workman. He hollows out new chambers
of joy to abide in, when he is gone.[1]

"He looked steadily at the ultimate,
not the immediate, reward"
(Heb. 11:26, Phillips).

6

Desolate Terrain? Exciting Journey?

"The way is easy and hard, joyful and full of terrors, ec-
static and suffering, sweet in the mouth, bitter in the belly,
bearing a cross in one hand and a crown in the other." [2]

He says it well. Sometimes it's misery. Sometimes fun.
Last week, fair skies . . . now discouraging clouds and dark
sounds in my soul.

Handling this ambivalence of mood takes some doing.
For me, both living today and long-range acceptance make
the mix. But when I am thinking straightest, I know my
commitment has no end. Too many years I lived on the giddy
edge of false hope: One day when I had my weight down, I
could go back to eating anything, everything, endlessly. In
this frame of mind every diet was like a prison sentence. I
looked forward with enthusiasm to freedom. To which most
fatties would chorus a loud Amen.

It is a great day for us when we conquer this kind of
dreaming. Much as we hate to face it, we will probably

---

1. Author unknown.
2. Thomas Powers, *First Questions on the Life of the Spirit* (New York: Harper &
Row, 1959), p. 55.

never hear, "Well done thou good and faithful servant. Eat like crazy."

Always over the door of our true release is a sign which reads, "Thin thinking must be sustained indefinitely."

So, what can we do? One answer is to concentrate on the excitement. When we take a positive attitude toward our problem, even world travel pales before the thrill of new discoveries inside ourselves. This is for sure: Accepting this challenge with zest, we will never be bored.

The mystics have some great terms for it. They call it "casting off the mantle of our misery" or "affirming our struggle."

In this light, taking our problem to heart can be good or bad, depending on us. If it means glooming and glumming and loving morbidity, that's bad. But we can never take anything too much to heart if that means carrying it to the Inner Presence.

* * * * * * *

AFFIRMATION: Today I take my eyes off the problem and focus them on my Lord. He knows how to turn desolate terrain into high country.

We are to look for the Divine Presence not so much in sudden extraordinary inrushes and miraculous bestowals, as in the processes which transform our stubborn nature.[3]

---

3. Rufus Jones, *Inner Life* (New York: Macmillan, 1916), p. 110.

After starvation a typical pattern
was to follow prescribed diets for a short
time, but then at some time
justify excessive eating because of life
stresses, a family celebration
or the fact that they were . . . below
top weight.[1]

7
Excuses, Excuses!

"And the man said, The woman whom thou gavest to be with me, she gave me of the tree, and I did eat" (Gen. 3:12).

We were waiting for some friends in a motel restaurant. Obviously, it was the place to eat in town. One of those alluring buffets, set up to wreck the strongest resolution. The customers came in all sizes and shapes. And we overheard this interesting conversation. One ample young businessman said to his friends, "I really ought to order from the menu. I can't help stuffing myself at these things."

Whereupon came the familiar barrage, "Oh, come on, Ken, live a little. We've really been hitting it hard this morning. You deserve it. This is no place to diet. Look at that fried chicken, man. All you can eat."

So Ken ate. And we may too under these people pressures. In any crowd we can count on it: There will be somebody near to ruin our resolves! Aunt Helen, maybe.

---

1. David W. Swanson, M.D., and Frank A. Dinello, Ph.D., "Follow-up of Patients Starved for Obesity," *Psychosomatic Medicine,* March-April 1970, p. 212.

She majors in strawberry pie and looks so wounded if we turn her down. Mrs. B, the nervous flibbertigibbet at the church dinners who can't take *no*.

I have even excused my eating for this absurdity: I must keep everyone happy. But that isn't true, and I know it. Most people could care less. They aren't really interested in what I eat. Generally, they're busy with their own selections. And if that isn't true, there is one thing I'd better remember: People are more interested in what I think of them than what they think of me. So here is one more place to quit kidding.

Adam and Eve are actual people to some readers of the Bible. To others they symbolize man's recognition of himself as a spiritual creature. But by any interpretation their story is familiar. And Adam's excuse of Genesis 3:12 is well known to some of us. We have our own versions: "They insisted I eat their smorgasbord." "I just couldn't insult the hostess." "My wife is a superb cook." "This woman thou gavest me."

Yet it always comes out the same way. It's my body, and what I feed it is up to me!

Between the first man and his Maker, that's how it was. God established early that we are responsible for some things with no excuses. Whether we like it or not is purely academic. Though *we* may not count it this time, our bodies will. Somewhere in our cells and molecules an internal computer files it away. That's how it is between the Lord and us. We may dodge, we may duck, we may hide or run, but he will find us. And when he does, the question to Adam is our question: "Have you eaten of that which I commanded you not to eat?"

****

Today's prayer is made up of selections from Psalms 54–59. The so-called Hate Psalms were pointed toward the enemies of Israel. Some scholars have suggested that their lack of worth to the modern Bible reader warrants removal from Scripture. But choosing various phrases makes them a potent prayer for those of us who must struggle against strong inner adversaries.

Hear my prayer, O God; give ear to the words of my mouth. . . . My soul is among lions. . . . They have prepared a net for my steps . . . they have digged a pit before me. Deliver me, O my God. . . . Defend me from them that rise up against me . . . for, lo, they lie in wait for my soul. . . . The mighty are gathered against me. . . . They return at evening: they make a noise like a dog, and go round about the city . . . wander up and down for meat, and grudge if they be not satisfied. Scatter them by thy power and let them know that God ruleth. *Amen.*

WHAT TO DO: For the next thirty days, every time I catch myself making an excuse, I will ask, "Is this a reason or an alibi?"

> Christians who excuse their own mediocrity with pious rationalizations seem guilty of not understanding the extent of God's call on their lives.[2]

2. Mark O. Hatfield, *Conflict and Conscience* (Waco, Texas: Word Books, 1971), p. 126.

8
Two Words for Temptation

"God is faithful, and he will not let you be tempted beyond your strength, but with the temptation will also provide the way of escape, that you may be able to endure it" (1 Cor. 10:13, RSV).

Grandpa and grandson were running through the pasture, chased by an enraged bull. "Grandpa," shouted the boy, "shouldn't we stop and pray?" To which the wise old sage answered, "Run like the dickens, sonny. I keep prayed up ahead for times like this."

Some battles are won far back of the front lines. As overeaters, we don't need to wait for the showdown. By prayer, by study, by resolve we can make some important decisions ahead of time.

I call it *pre-think* and it is one of two vital words for me in handling temptation.

Adequate pre-think has to be right because that's how God does it. The Apostle Paul tells us in today's verse that God has already done his part. He has made sure that the

29

odds are not beyond our capacity. This idea that there is help going ahead of us is a tremendous truth for anyone. And it takes on special meaning for the obese and overweight.

But God can't do it alone, and my second key word is *speed*. The sooner I turn down what I shouldn't eat, the better. Pondering only makes it harder. This is true because rationalizing for me tips heavy on the side of lies and half-truths. I know there are many places where I should not make quick judgments. Sometimes I must think things through. But debating about my eating is never a time for dallying.

One day when I was studying the story of Jesus' temptation, I saw these same two things. Even the casual reader will note that hunger came first. The use of the sensational to attract crowds was there. Using his powers to build his own kingdom was a part of it also. But the number one lure offered by the tempter was something to eat. And the serious student, fat or thin, can't miss these two facts: Jesus was well fortified with pre-think. He met the temptation with words learned long before the struggle began. Then he acted with speed. He wasted no time taking his stand.

Blessed is he who comes to temptation well prepared. Blessed also is he who takes the offensive at once.

* * * * * * *

This is the nature of Christian self-denial . . . this kind cannot be grabbed at in a moment of temptation . . . such moments only reveal whether you have it or not.[1]

1. Robert Raines, *Creative Brooding* (New York: Macmillan, 1965), p. 43.

9

No Day Is a Bad Day to Begin

"Now is the good time. Now is the day" (2 Cor. 6:2, The New Testament in Basic English).

Very fine thinking here from Corinthians. For some people.

I've known groups working on the weight problem who built this day-at-a-time concept into their program. But to my kind of mind it carries a grave danger. By overconcentrating on one twenty-four-hour period, I may expect too much. Today I must sacrifice. I know that, and I won't mind today. But tomorrow those beautiful calorie-laden foods will be back. Let me at them.

Of course, such thinking is ridiculous. But when I am in this frame of mind, here's what happens. If I have ten pounds to lose, I'm sure to be disappointed. Why didn't I lose them all yesterday on my Spartan dedication? One-fourth pound. One-half. One. That's hardly a dent in my great mountain. So, true to the fat man's mental maneuvers, I start to resent what I ought to be celebrating.

31

Always, this tricky business is germane to our struggle. We are the searchers for simple solutions. We dream of easy methods. We fantasize, "I've got enough problems, see? What I want is some quick answers."

So, although I hate to admit it, "One day at a time" is probably not for me. I must quit dangling false hopes of total freedom. Permanent liberty may be one more "never."

The best thing I can say about today is: Settle down on this simple truth. *No day is a bad day to begin.*

10
The Sinister Trap of Doing Well

"Take heed lest you forget the Lord your God, by not keeping his commandments and his ordinances and his statutes, lest, when you have eaten and are full, then your heart be lifted up, and you forget the Lord your God" (Deut. 8:11-14, RSV).

Fritzy said a meaningful thing in his prayer. It was after a mammoth Thanksgiving dinner. Grandpa and grandma were there with numerous cousins and kinfolk. "Bless mommy and daddy," he started. Then he took off from there to enumerate the miscellaneous relatives who had stuffed themselves at the table. But he couldn't go on. With a huge little-boy sigh, he finished, "I guess I'll have to say goodnight, God. I'm just too full."

Our blessings can be too much. Many a person has lost his soul to his own success. Some of us know what the writer of Deuteronomy means. As the pounds come off, we tend to let up on our commitment.

Why?

One answer is that success of any kind is not only beautiful, it is also dangerous. Prosperity is fun. It excites us. But it may also blind us to some sinister traps. These come standard equipment on every model. But for the dieter, they could have grave consequences.

Here then are some moments when we need to be especially on guard.

1. When our scales begin to move downward. The closer it gets to our appointed weight loss, the more we should set up our guards.

2. When our clothes begin to indicate that we are doing well in reshaping our contour. Fact: Every time we win a battle we are tempted to think we have won the war.

3. When we are taking a few nibbles we wouldn't have taken yesterday or last week.

4. When people begin to praise us for what we have accomplished. We should want to look good to others, but more than that, how are we looking in God's sight?

5. When we begin to compare ourselves with others who aren't doing as well. The fatties around us can be an ever present danger.

6. When we begin to reward ourselves with forbidden foods. Some of our favorites have got to go forever.

Genuine satisfaction deep inside can be heaven sent. Excessive pride is the devil's wedge.

ANOTHER WORTHY WORD FOR TODAY'S MEDITATION: "And they took strong cities, and a fat land, and possessed houses full of all goods, wells digged, vineyards, and oliveyards, and fruit trees in abundance: so they did eat, and were filled, and became fat" (Neh. 9:25).

I will give you several counsels. If you
are able to fast you will do well . . . for
in addition to the ordinary benefits
of fasting, namely elevating the
spirit, subduing the flesh, strengthening
virtue . . . it is a great matter
to be able to command our tastes and
inclinations, and to keep the
body and its appetites subject to the
law of the spirit.[1]

11
Fasting

*"And he said unto them, This kind can come forth by
nothing, but by prayer and fasting"* (Mark 9:29).

Effective fasting has a long history. Both Old Testament
and New make positive claims for it. In this Scripture, Jesus
tells us that some things will require drastic handling.

In the fat person's commitment pace is all important. It
is possible to become confused about inner directions. Sometimes what we think is divine guidance could be a false
voice from some crack in our id. Resignation needs constant
checking for the authentic. This is one reason why fasting
should always be supervised by a doctor.

Most of the medics these days take a dim view of fasting
for long periods. The reason is that we may be losing what
we ought not to lose.

In research at the medical libraries, I found the experts
sounding this note often, "Body composition studies have

---

1. Francis De Sales (1567–1622), *A Diary of Meditations* (Chicago: Henry Reg-
nery Co., 1957), p. 33.

indicated that in complete starvation, 66 percent of the total weight loss was fat-free tissue." [2]

Which being interpreted in laymen's language waves this red flag: We should only be 34 percent pleased for what we lose by fasting over an extended period.

One of my doctor friends says, "For the first three days, your body processes will be consuming only fat. You may even have a bit of euphoric reaction which stimulates. What's going on inside is like small amounts of alcohol in the system. It gives you a feeling of relaxation and well-being. Then after the third day, this comes to a halt and another process starts. Now the hunger begins gnawing away at essential materials."

After much supervised experimentation, I have found it exactly like they say. My body begins to give off warning signals, and I get the message, "That's enough."

So here's a suggestion for those who may want to try it. Three days fasting, two days eating; or two days fasting, one day eating. Then repeat the process till you come to your right size.

Such a procedure may be particularly helpful when we have dieted our way down to what doctors call "fat pockets" or "fat deposits." I call it suet and that means the hard stuff.

But, run that warning by again! Fasting is not recommended without supervision. And even then, we must remember that weight loss in big blocks is not likely to be as permanent as steady loss in the aggregate. Generally, the word for us is evolution, not revolution.

Then there is another background requirement even more serious than the first. We might as well forget it until we have ourselves well psyched out. The doctors with exten-

2. George E. Scharf, M.D., "Diet and Management of Obesity," *American Journal of Clinical Nutrition,* March 1971, p. 287.

sive experience in this field are in unanimous agreement. Very few fasters hold their loss permanently. This being true, we might as well face it. Fasting without understanding our neuroses dead-ends in misery. We may be temporarily elated with the pounds we have lost. But when they're back on, we will be carrying heavier burdens—guilt and shame and self-disdain.

When Jesus talks about prayer and fasting, he has the right order. First comes the kind of prayer which searches our history for hidden causes. Always the prelude for us is ruthless honesty.

The Hebrew word for fasting signifies the humble submission of the soul to God. Jesus did not abolish fasting; He lifted it from the legalism of the Old Covenant into the freedom of the New. Fasting is an outward act, which should be carried out when there is an inner need.[3]

THOUGHT FOR MEDITATION: "The stag runs badly alike when it is too fat and when it is too thin, and we are exposed to temptation when the body is over-indulged and when it is over-subdued; for as the one makes it easy and indolent, so the other makes it low and desponding . . . those who have begun with over-strictness at last are compelled to be over-lax. Would it not have been better to keep strictly to such an even-ordered system as was suitable? . . . continued, habitual temperance is far better than occasional rigid abstinence alternated with great relaxation." [4]

3. O. Hallesby, *Prayer* (Minneapolis: Augsburg, 1931), p. 112.
4. De Sales, *A Diary of Meditations.*

12
Meet Me on the Hill

"He himself endured a cross . . . because of the joy he knew would follow" (Heb. 12:2, Phillips).

Same song, next verse, and forever. There is no easy way. By his word, his action, Jesus made this plain. Only when we have gone "to the cross" can we know the joy of victory.

Always in a serious prayer life there will be certain echoes. And one of these is the answer to our prayer, "Today I want to live your way." Loud and clear the reply comes: "It's a date. Meet me on the hill."

This tough road to the cross is a sure part of our commitment but like the writer of Hebrews tells us, "The joy follows."

I have a list in my notebook labeled, "What I am getting by giving up."

1. *I am getting my self-respect.* I really do like me better when I am living God's way. Pride may be bad when it's false pride. But there is another kind which is all good. This is the pride I feel when I am true to my commitment.

2. *I am getting my body in shape.* I like what I see in the mirror when I am slimming down. He knows and I know how good I feel when I am sizing up right.

3. *I am getting a longer time to live.* Doctors tell me it is so and my insurance man agrees. Sobering statistics these: "For every ten to fifteen pounds you carry too long, you give up a couple of years on your chances." I like to eat. I love it. But doesn't it stand to reason? I really can eat more if I live longer!

4. *I am getting an alertness of body and mind.* Heavy head goes with heavy body. When I let go my wants, I feel some great new things. Vitality. Spirit. Vigor. These too I gain by giving up.

5. *I am getting myself into a position to help others.* Everyone I meet is in need of God's love. Family. Friends. Fellow workers. Known. Unknown. No exceptions. There is a kind of theological chic which says, "God could get along fine without you. Don't be so presumptuous." I can't accept that. God put me here for his reasons. One of these is to love. When I have bowed to his will, I am better able to reach out.

6. *I am getting one thing more, and this is the greatest. When I yield to what I know he wants, I have set my foot on the road to his true joy.*

Whenever we pray and mean it, "Lord, today I want to live with you," his answer comes clear: "It's a date. Meet me on the hill."

The tough road to Calvary is a sure part of Christian commitment. Jesus didn't like it, and we won't. But that's how it is. Christian joy has no detours.

"He himself endured a cross . . . because of the joy he knew would follow."

II

I Look inside Me

Introduction

Psychiatrists are nice people. I don't see how they take it, listening eight hours a day, sometimes more. Most of them are kind and wise. Now and then I meet one who looks like he should have bananas behind his ears. Every bit as neurotic as I am. But I will forever be grateful for their contribution to my recovery.

For eight years I sat where they sat. I was on the board of a psychiatric hospital in one of America's major cities. They had me there, I think, for an interesting reason. Many of them sensed that religion and health go together. I listened as they read their papers. I heard them discuss specific cases. Some of what they said was too much for me. But this came through loud and clear, "Most of what we are today was shaped way back there in our history!"

Some may need only a little psyching out for return to right proportions. Others require a lot of it—I did. But where I found my help was not in the doctor's office. Instead I went to the medical libraries and dug in. The reason I went at it this way is that I didn't know where else to go. My psychiatrist friends seemed to divide themselves into some distinct classifications.

Some were skinny.

Others were so gross they obviously hadn't solved their own problems.

And then there were those who were just right. But among these I couldn't find a single one with any real sensitivity to my problem. So I decided to begin serious research into a vast medical storehouse on the psychology of obesity.

No matter where you live, you probably aren't too far from this kind of help. Your doctor can point you in the right direction. Usually this will be in a large medical center. (You might need help from an M.D. for permission to use these facilities.)

Most librarians conduct themselves with a "hush" which makes them seem unapproachable. But don't let it fool you. Once you break through this sound barrier, you may find a real friend. The librarian will show you the index and explain how to use it. Under the heading of obesity, diet, fasting, nutrition, and a number of other good words you'll find some fascinating titles. Make your list and head for the stacks.

Did you know that there are more than fifteen hundred medical journals in publication? I didn't. What I discovered was that every field of medicine has some interest in our problem. Gynecology. Surgery. Obstetrics. Pediatrics. Orthopedics. Urology. And all the rest. There are few exceptions. And the whole thing became like an exciting game. From rows and rows of these bound volumes, I sleuthed my way to some real help. Any person who undertakes this kind of serious study can make some great discoveries for himself. Down subterranean roads he will begin to see the "why" of his excess poundage.

Self-research may be our best approach for several reasons. For one thing, we are with ourselves 100 percent of the time. Consultation with a psychiatrist can seldom be more than once or twice a week. In self-study we can work at it constantly.

Then too, what we do for ourselves gives us a dignity we won't get any other way.

If you need a professional, run, don't walk to the nearest phone. But if you are only part kookie like I was, this new approach may be for you.

* * * * * * *

"Whence comes it that the vessel does not sail? Is it that there is no wind? No, the breath of heaven never fails, but the vessel is held fast by anchors that we do not perceive: they are at the bottom of the deep."[1]

---

1. Francois Fénelon (1651–1715), *Letters and Reflections* (New York: World Publishing Co., 1955), p. 100.

1
Unbraiding Our Brains

"Search me, O God, and know my heart: try me, and know my thoughts: And see if there be any wicked way in me, and lead me in the way everlasting" (Ps. 139:23–24).

For years I tried to get a lean body on a fat mind. Sometimes I had a bit of success. I ground off a few pounds by iron determination. But it was a surface loss. Down deep the heavy problems were still there. And that's how it is. Before we can get the fat off our framework, we must get it out of our heads.

Accepting the shape we're in will forever be step one. Step two must be a fearless search for reasons. *Something* made us kinky inside.

We didn't come this way from the Maker. Forces over which we had no control at the time tangled the designs. People who meant well but didn't know better had an effect on us. Mistakes of our own doing, the choices we made—all these played a part in shaping us. And before we can look right again, we must go back to the original.

The personality boys are fond of saying, "Nobody is as interesting to the individual as himself." Nice thought, but not altogether true. If we stick to the surface and regions immediately below it, yes! But down in the lower self there are snarls and knots and confused patterns. And for most of us these are frightening. Yet there is no escape from this truth: Flabby waistline means there has been some flabby thinking.

In today's Scripture, the writer goes at it properly. He prays for God's help to find what needs reworking: "Search me." He prays for divine wisdom in testing the possibilities: "Try me." He prays for insight to face his full responsibility: "See if there be any wicked way in me." He asks God to take his hand and guide him to permanent recovery: "Lead me in the way everlasting."

Good prayer, and it's for me. So is any prayer which leads to total honesty inside.

Every wise counselor to the overweight advises, "Go to your doctor."

That's good advice.

We should listen to our medics. We should study everything we can on the physical side. Knowledge of the body and its intricate wonders is important. We do well to learn foods and diets and how they affect us.

But this is only part of our problem. *Always, the lasting solution is down under.*

Woeful truth, and scary: Scratch a fat man and you will find a neurotic. So that's how it stands. We can never get a lean body on a fat mind, permanently.

****

"Clearly, achievement of weight loss should not be utilized as the end point of therapy, but rather treatment of the basic underlying emotional problems must be incorporated into the program." [1]

---

1. "Obesity: A Continuing Enigma," editorial from the *Journal of the American Medical Association*, January 1970.

2
Are You Kidding, Jeremiah?

"Seek me, and you shall find me; when you seek for me with all your heart, I will reveal myself to you" (Jer. 29:13, Moffatt).

I once saw an interesting sign at the foot of a mountain. It listed the needs for the climb and made some suggestions. It detailed the various routes and gave a time schedule. Then as a sign-off warning, it asked, "Are you sure you're ready?"

Good question for the fat man. Woman too. Most of us have been here time after time. We've said it with meaning, "This time I mean business." But though our mind said yes, our heart said half a no. And soon we were back with our purposes dragging.

Jeremiah tells it like it is. The true finder of God must be a true seeker. We must come to God with all our defenses down. A study of Jeremiah's early life turns up this interesting background. He probably came from a setting where things were rather nice. Yet deep in his heart he felt the call to service. That wouldn't be easy in a day like his. In

48

fact, it would be downright dismal at times. And like he does with us, God seemed to keep testing, testing. Are you sure, Jeremiah? Or are you kidding?

In their literature on the psychology of obesity, medical authorities sound this note:

> Weight reduction usually should be postponed until the patient has the requisite psychological strength and self-understanding.
>
> In my experience, the massively obese patient has massive psychological problems.
>
> Although diet and exercise always will be basic to any program of weight reduction, they can be used most effectively when the patient understands what has caused the overweight.[1]

The doctor says it well. Until we are prepared to face the truth, we might as well forget reducing. Most of us heavies have been excellent starters. And the majority have one poor ending for every good beginning. This we don't need again.

So here is the burning question from physician and climber and Jeremiah, "Are you sure you're ready?"

* * * * * * *

"All Christian religion wholly consisteth in this, to learn to know ourselves: whence we are come, and what we are; how we have stirred up these evils in us; and how we may recover our original blessedness." [2]

---

1. Robert S. Weinhaus, M.D., "The Management of Obesity: Some Recent Concepts," *Journal of the Missouri State Medical Association*, September 1969.
2. Jacob Boehme, *The Way to Christ*, written in the 1600s, p. 125.

"He must grow greater, but I must grow less" (John 3:30, Weymouth).

3
Good-by to the Grandiose Me

"The psychoanalysis of obese patients reveals a grave distortion of their sense of reality. A common trait is the feeling of being 'special,' of having to be bigger and better than anybody else. . . . Once the fat person decides on reducing, he approaches it with the same 'all or nothing' attitude that characterizes his other unrealistic goals. The cautious calculations which a physician may offer are far below his plan of achieving slimness in a much shorter time and more dramatic way. . . . It is unavoidable that with such an attitude a person suffers one defeat after another and lives in an atmosphere of frustration and anxiety." [1]

That's what they all say. The overweight mind forever plays tricks. And one of the slickest is this: If we can't be great, we can at least be big. Sounds silly. Way out. Ludicrous. But here's one fatty who would have to say, "When I quit laughing, I found tricky maneuvers in me."

---

1. Hilde Bruch, "The Psychosomatic Aspects of Obesity," *Journal of the Mount Sinai Hospital,* 20:1.

I first caught on one night at a county fair. We were watching the man guessing weights. "Step right up, folks. Only one little, thin, skinny coin. If I miss you ten pounds, I give you a Kewpie doll." For a long time we studied his expertise and noticed one thing. He would miss most often on the fat folks. His biggest margin of error was a huge junior-high boy. Pitiful creature, really. And I was about to observe so when I felt this tug on my jacket. "Daddy," she said, "see, he always misses people like you. Win me a Kewpie doll."

You would think I'd have learned. But the *other* person looks so gross to me. Undisciplined. I measure the world by one standard and me by another.

Everyone in the world is somebody special. This is the unique claim of our faith. Nobody is second rate with God. But if we are overweighers, we better check for the delusion that we are special-special. Under the layers somewhere there is probably a false sense of importance.

We know John was talking about spiritual things when he said, "He must grow greater and I must grow less." But sometimes the Scripture has special applications, and this one is right on our target. Somewhere we got the wrong idea: We were one of God's favorite people. . . . Never you worry. . . . He would exempt us. So we grew and grew the wrong way.

Some time if we are to recover, we must reverse the order. Away at the center that's how it is, "I must decrease and he must increase."

4
But I Also Don't Like Me

"Reproach hath broken my heart; and I am full of heaviness" (Ps. 69:20).

Self-love isn't all of our problem.

The special-special thing in most of us leads to another ugly: self-condemnation. The higher our phony standards, the lower we go when we fail to meet them. Most obese and overweight know a thousand different tunes to "I Hate Me." Side by side with our high self-regard runs a deep reproach for our countless failures. We know what the psalmist meant. Behind our heavy contours is a heavy, heavy heart.

Some of this comes from infancy. If we were fat children, we were constantly exposed to derogatory comments. If we escaped them at home, they came from playground, schoolroom, neighbors, relatives. Raised eyebrows, pointed fingers, continuous insult are a part of our overweight history. Which for a hapless youngster leads always to the same grim end—personal rejection with self-incrimination.

The psychiatric literature explains what happens in this battle between "special-special" and "I hate me." It also shows us clearly how our eating is affected. Until we bring these conflicting forces to the peace table, they may be making us hungry.

From the same writer who explains grandiosity come these words on its exact opposite:

> The gulf between the aspiration level which is impossibly high and the person's inability to live up to his ambition is so great that he has to resort to some means of alleviating the tension and despair. In fat people overeating is the most important means of relieving the felt dissatisfaction. It fulfills the primitive hope that eating will make up for the defect. Yet, however much food they take, eating never gives the satisfaction they really want to feel; it does not accomplish the very special thing they want to accomplish.[1]

False goals are a real part of the fat person's problem. Thinking of ourselves as the finest, we expect the finest from us. Which isn't so bad, to a point. But we'd better be realistic. To strain for the unrealistic makes us nervous. This kind of tension we do not need.

And that isn't all. False goals unachieved bring an exaggerated feeling of guilt. When we fail to meet our expectations, we abuse ourselves and scold unduly. True, most of this takes place in the subconscious. But it's all very real and every bit deadly.

Some psychiatrists say that overeating can even stem from a hidden death wish. Gourmandizing, they tell us, is one of the most socially acceptable routes to suicide. I have studied this theory in depth. And you should too if you think it applies. But I guess the reason it has never reached me is this: I have convinced myself that the longer I live,

---

1. Hilde Bruch, "The Psychosomatic Aspects of Obesity."

the more I can eat. That seems to be more of my problem than digging my grave at the dinner table.

Complicated, isn't it? Very involved. We overeat when we hate ourselves. And we hate ourselves when we overeat.

So, how do we get off this merry-go-round? For some of us the answer is spiritual. God alone can break our heart's anger. We must bring it to him and ask for his clarity. We must surrender our phony self-image and pray for a God-given tolerance.

****

PRAYER: Lord, reproach has broken my heart and I am full of heaviness. Clarify my goals and show me what you want. Help me to quit beating myself for my failures.

Without your guidance, I become overangry when I see myself still so imperfect. I know that some kind of interior humiliation is good. But some is only a contortion of false guilt. Make me humble where I should be, but show me when to stop.

Teach me how to reprove myself without anger and bitterness. I want to recognize sickness, but I don't want to wallow in it. *Amen.*

****

QUESTION FOR TODAY: Are there forces in my history still pushing me beyond what's natural for me?

Do I face personal shortcoming realistically or take self-anger out in my eating?

Are my goals based on good sense or fantasy?

5
Scare Tactics

*"Do you know that you are God's temple and that God's
spirit dwells in you? . . . For God's temple is holy, and that
temple you are"* (1 Cor. 3:16–17, RSV).

There is little wonder that the obese do not live to a ripe
old age. . . . they suffer more severely than their normal
weight fellows from hardening of the arteries, high blood
pressure, pulmonary disease, pancreatic troubles, and a host of
other diseases. . . . The heart suffers as it is required to
pump blood through an additional two-thirds mile of blood
vessels for every pound of added fat. . . . Excessive fat inter-
feres with the mechanical efficiency of all the vital organs.
. . . Some liver disfunction is always detectable by simple
tests upon the blood. . . . the kidney is the last of the vital
organs to show changes directly due to overweight. However,
that it is physiologically handicapped there can be no doubt.[1]

Obesity shortens life proportionally to weight and age . . .

---

1. Thomas Hodge McGavack, M.D., quoted in *U.S. News and World Report*, 28
August 1961, from an article "Latest on Being Overweight and What to Do about
It."

the longer the duration of obesity, the worse is the life out-look . . . that the increased weight must handicap the me-chanics of the skeletal structure is obvious, not only through the effect of the sheer weight itself, but the center of gravity is changed . . . there are a number of consequences of an orthopedic variety . . . one of the commonest is bilateral arthritis. This is proven by its alleviation when a considerable loss in weight is attained.[2]

The vice-president of one of the country's leading invest-ment banks advised, "Do not invest in companies run by fat men . . ." for each five pounds above ideal weight life ex-pectancy is reduced by about one year.[3]

Ho hum! So what else is new?

Scare tactics all affect me the same way, zero. Ditto for my fat friends. Always, mortality statistics have a remote tabular effect on us. Whatever startling impact they register, it soon fades away.

Thank you, doctor, for your concern. But if you mean your statistics to rattle our peace, cool it. We may frighten temporarily. Like thirty minutes, twenty-four hours, a week, or six.

But there are several reasons why these horror stories fail to give us the shivers. One is that obesity carries with it that aura of self-exemption. As we have already seen, *we are among the favorites.*

Here's another thing which draws a yawn at the pointing fingers. It may be true that gluttony makes dull and un-responsive people. But we even like our semistupor some times. Aches and awkwardness come on slow. So, too, does the really bad stuff that gets to our vital organs. We're living

---

2. Eli Moschcowitz, M.D., "Essays on the Biology of Disease," *Journal of the Mount Sinai Hospital,* 11:357.
3. Robert S. Weinhaus, M.D., "The Management of Obesity: Some Recent Con-cepts," *Journal of the Missouri State Medical Association,* September 1969, p. 719.

for pleasure, remember? And what is so pleasant as food? Nothing, except more food.

Besides we've been pushed into dieting too much for mortality statistics to be effective anymore. Long ago we closed the door to anyone who intrudes on our privacy. Pushy people in our background are one of the reasons for all this padding. Why? Why does it work this way? We don't know for sure and maybe we never will. But you won't scare us with the somber stuff.

Of course, there are a few unusual circumstances which might create an exception. One of my friends has a built-in timer, a stomach hernia. When he eats too much, the big meals press down and make him violently ill. Others have gastric reactions to heavy feeding. But I also could name you a bunch who get an opposite reaction. Their hurts come when they start to lose weight.

Saul of Tarsus was a fighter. He fought people. He fought God. He fought Saul. His problems were physical, mental, spiritual. He was out to set the world right. And it took a blinding experience to turn him around. Nobody knows for sure all of these inner conflicts. But this is for certain. Saul only recovered when he came to a new concept of himself. In today's verse he admits to a higher reference and calls us to do the same. He had hurt people in all good conscience. He had hurt Saul without knowing what he was doing. But hurting the new ruler of his life simply would not do.

That's how it must be for us. Nobody is going to tell us what to eat or how much we should weigh! But suddenly in Paul's blindness he sensed that life did not belong to *him*.

In the final analysis we come back to this core truth: We are out of shape because we are out of touch with the original.

... during trials the feelings
of piety are not lost; they only disappear
from sight, hiding themselves
at the bottom of the soul,
often beneath their exact opposite.
They shelter there, they purify
themselves and become strong and they
emerge from time to time
with a new vigour.[1]

6

Workmen in the Unawareness

"In due season we shall reap, if we faint not" (Gal. 6:9).

The most meaningful changes in me often take place in my unawareness. Now and then comes a flash of insight. Fresh. Sparkling. This new discovery excites me. Then mysteriously it seems to slip away.

I think I know where it goes. Weeks later, more likely months, I suddenly sense my life is different. Some tension is gone, some hammer laid away. Without my knowing it, some of the troubles have disappeared. I may not have sensed their going, but somehow I feel better.

To wait on these inner adjustments is not always easy for the obese and overweight. We want it done fast. Hurry up now! But the writer of Galatians is reminding us that utopia never arrives special delivery tomorrow. Like every other good thing, success only comes "in due season." And the next four words are the hooker, "if we faint not."

This is another of our major problems. All fatties are prone to want something for nothing.

---

1. Jean Pierre DeCaussade (1675–1751), *On Prayer* (Springfield, Ill.: Templegate, 1964), p. 129.

Yet, this is not what God promises. When we really get on his wave length, we hear a different note. Now the message is, "Give me an honest effort. I'll take your commitment and work it through even without your knowing. You be faithful and one day you will know that I have been faithful too."

So now when I get a flash of new discovery, I will think on it. I'll keep it around as long as it holds my interest. Try it out a little bit maybe, but mostly I pray, "Lord, here it is. I'm giving it now to you. Put it where you know I need it inside me. Use it. I'll wait."

****

THOUGHTS ON DELAYED REACTION: "For the moment all discipline seems painful rather than pleasant; later it yields the peaceful fruit of righteousness to those who have been trained by it" (Heb. 12:11, RSV).

"Plant patience in the garden of your soul. The roots are bitter, but the fruits are sweet" (author unknown).

We begin now a series of
six studies on a delicate theme. Nearly
all writers on our problem
take us back to the mother-child
relationships. Until we analyze these,
they say, we may be eating
for false reasons.
If you will pray for insight,
and not be repulsed too quickly,
you might be in for a blessing. Facing
the bad you have never faced,
you may come to some good
you have never known.

7

Mother's Food–The Oral Syndrome

Classic statement from long-gone sage: "The researches of
so many eminent scientific men have thrown so much dark-
ness on our subject that if they continue we shall soon know
nothing at all."

Say it again! Say it loud and clear about our problem.
There are many mysteries here. And one of the fuzziest
deals with the oral syndrome. They write about it often in
the literature and some of it is over our heads. But what
can we comprehend that might be helpful?

Let's begin right here—we *love* to eat!

Others may get their prime satisfactions elsewhere. For
us it goes in right here . . . over our teeth, around our
tongue, warm, cold, any way, every way! Lots of it!

That, say the wise men, is our problem. "Love" for us
must be something going in at the mouth. Others might
be satisfied with a full stomach. But not you and me. We
care too much for feel and taste and that makes us oral
characters.

In the psychological literature we come on frequent references to this phase of our problem:

The child experiences the first relief from discomfort during nursing. Thus, the satisfaction of hunger becomes deeply associated with the feeling of well being. . . . Another important emotional connection is that between sucking and pleasurable sensations in the mucous membrane of the mouth, lips, and tongue.[1]

Available evidence seems to indicate that these patients do not derive satisfaction from the relief of hunger. As a result, they look for reassurance. They have the desire to test the breast again and are driven to a compulsive repetition of the experience of being fed.[2]

Sorting out our mother memories is a gigantic assignment. On the one side we are steeped in mother reverence. "Good old mom." "That silver haired mother of mine." "Hushabye, rockabye." These were drilled into us as children and time never eases the pressure.

Psychiatrists call this the "Mother Syndrome." Which being interpreted means our mother was a "heavy." She may have been beautiful, good, generous, kind. She may be living today or only a distant memory. But if we carry too many pounds, this theme is worth our study.

Certain of the literature is sickening and sick. There are writers on the theme who have never recovered from their own version of a negative "momism." Some of my psychiatrist friends leave me with the impression, "If you could only hate your mother enough, everything would be just dandy."

I don't believe it. Mine did the best she could with her problems. And they were many, including me. But I have

---

1. Arthur Kornhaber, M.D., "The Stuffing Syndrome," *Psychosomatics*, November–December 1970.
2. H. A. Thorner, "On Compulsive Eating," *Journal of Psychosomatic Research*, 1970, vol. 14, p. 325.

learned that the men of the mind are right about this—my compulsive obsessive drives are often mother oriented.

Eating is in the beginning a matter of two people—the feeding adult and the eating newborn. This brings us to another symbolic aspect of food—namely, its motherliness. Feeding is not only kindly and warm in its emotional meaning to the one who accepts, but he is most likely to see the giver as somehow glossed with the meaning of "mother." [3]

3. Karl Menninger, *Love Against Hate* (New York: Harcourt, Brace and World, 1942), p. 273.

8
Mother's Food–The Longing for Love

Here begins a long list. In my twenty-year pilgrimage to better proportion I have met a host of fellow travelers. Beautiful people, most of them. Struggling hard as I was. They have enriched my life with numerous insights.

From these sources comes a series of "Mother" questions which might be worth musing.

CHECK QUESTION 1. *Are we eating to fill gaps which never can be filled with food?*

Every human being comes from his Maker with an inner vacuum, waiting to be filled with real love. The emotionally healthy home intends to fill these reservoirs adequately. Parents, family, church, school, neighbors, friends are all a part of this input. Marriage adds to the supply, and each year should find fresh inflow from many sources.

But sometimes that's not how it is. At any given point our love openings may be blocked. In even the best homes, intake doors are sometimes closed. They are closed by us.

They are closed by others. They are closed for reasons unknown. Yet the gaps are no less real and they need to be understood where possible. And where they cannot be understood, this can: *Heavy eating as a love search is futile!*

There are parents who cannot love properly no matter how hard they try. With some mothers, all available energies are drained off in their own neurotic trends.

Carrying a grudge against a mother like this only aggravates the problem. If ours was one of these, the solution is to face honestly our total mother history. Only when we have done this can we treat our problem with dignity. Then we can love her for all the good she did and accept her shortcomings with mercy. It requires a high level of maturity to research these sensitive areas. But the road to full recovery is a long road and it calls for courage.

Comes next a query for those unfortunate souls who grew up in a fighting family.

CHECK QUESTION 2: *Do the happiest memories focus at the dinner table?*

As one fellow struggler put it, "I hate to say this, but when I look back, I honestly think our main entertainment was seeing how mad we could make some member of the family. I hope we didn't hate each other all that much, but that's the way I remember. Whenever we sat down at the table, it was like everyone declared a temporary cessation of hostilities. Mom was a great cook. When mealtime came, we occupied ourselves with all her good food. And it always seemed to me like a very welcome truce."

So what can we do about this lack of love in our personal history? We can seek the wisdom of experts if we need it. And one thing more, we can force ourselves off the dead center of selfishness.

This is a constant threat to the fatty. Our obesity weighs so heavy on us, that we are taken up totally with our own problems. And unless we guard this, we become obsessed with our own needs. We forget that others have troubles too. It is a very healthy procedure for us to ask ourselves, "What can I do for someone else today?" Here is one fatty who has learned: The more time I take to help someone else, the more I am helped myself.

✹ ✹ ✹ ✹ ✹ ✹ ✹

VERSE FOR MEDITATION: "Give and it shall be given unto you" (Luke 6:38).

9

Mother's Food–Habits and Philosophy

CHECK QUESTION 3. *Did our mother know the facts about nutrition?*

"My mom thought a well-balanced meal was a piece of cake in one hand and a dish of ice cream in the other. . . ." "Mine was like that too. We were brought up on bread and butter, preserves and honey, potatoes, gravy, noodles, and things like that. Desserts were her specialty. I know she thought this was right. But it seems like I need a complete new dietary training. . . ." "My mother was so dominated by other people around her that her only self-expression was in culinary excess. We all loved it, and the more we told her, the more she poured it on. . . ." "It sure helped me when I studied my mother's attitude toward food and how I was letting it affect me. She urged us to eat, and eat, and eat. Until I realized this, I even felt anxious when I dieted. You know what I mean? I felt guilty as if I was injuring my mother. When I went home for my vacation, I always gained weight in order to give my mother the pleasure of overfeeding me." (Quotes from a dieters' prayer group)

CHECK QUESTION 4. *Was our mother overly proud of her well-fed children?*

Obese children are generally treated as a precious possession, overstuffed with food, and shielded from the ordinary demands and dangers of life by oversolicitous parents. . . . obese patients characteristically have a history of maladjustment in family relationships.[1]

Some writers propose an interesting theory. They say that the overfed child develops an excessive number of fat cells. This takes place early. It might even begin in babyhood. But according to the theory, these fat cells never go away. The argument is intended to admonish young mothers: Don't let your baby get too heavy.

For some of us it has another application. Our baby pictures may give us a clue. Or maybe Aunt Sophie can tell us how it was. And if we were roly-poly in infancy, this may tell us two things: (a) something about our mother's idea of nutrition; (b) that we will be forever faced with the necessity for double vigilance.

CHECK QUESTION 5. *Did we eat to the tune of clean your plate?*

One of the big things at our house was all this stuff about the poor people who didn't have enough to eat. I must have heard it a million times, "Think of the starving Chinese, or Indians, and a whole bunch of the emaciated hungry." When we heard this most was at mealtime until we were downright ashamed if we didn't eat the table bare.

Would you believe I picked up the idea as a kid that I was doing all these sad people a favor if I stuffed myself. Now isn't that ridiculous? (Another quote from a dieters' prayer group)

1. Arthur Dick, "Psychological Aspects of Obesity," *Medical Arts and Sciences,* third quarter, 1961, p. 97.

"But my mother told me it's bad manners to leave food on the plate!" "When did she tell you that?" "When I was eight years old and was being fattened up because I was so thin." Here the unconscious mother image is visible; an educational command is taken verbatim, and applied at the wrong place, with the wrong intention.[2]

My own clean-your-plate training came to a jarring re-think one unforgettable evening. Five children yammering around the dinner table do not always filter their chatter. This time they didn't. We had finished one of their mother's sumptuous meals. I had cleaned my plate thoroughly as my custom was. Now I was cleaning their plates as my custom was. But this evening while I was grazing on everyone's leftovers, one of the small fry observed, "You know, I just thought of something. If we didn't have daddy, we'd have to keep a pig." Close, so very close to what the psychiatrists call "garbage pail obesity."

CHECK QUESTION 6. *Were we brought up with a poverty complex?*

Get it while the getting is good. Tomorrow daddy may be losing his job. . . . See this steak, son. It will probably be the last you'll see for a long time.

Those from this background may be carrying an un-necessary low-grade concern. We may have been living like bears, stuffing ourselves for the lean winter days. And if that is our habit, here too our religion provides the answer. We do well to meditate on the abundance of God. There

---

2. Edmund Bergler, M.D., "Psychoanalytical Aspects of the Personality of the Obese Person," *International Record of Medicine*, January 1958, p. 7.

is healing in this promise of the Book, "My God shall supply all your needs." Note, the word is not wants, but needs.

✱✱✱✱✱✱✱

CONCLUSION: Those earliest food attitudes in our homes are worth studying. Eating is partly habit. Some habits have outlived their usefulness for today's well-being.

10
Mother's Food—Seduction and Control

CHECK QUESTION 7. *Are we freed of our mother's goals?*
Uncanny how many obese people I have known came
from a pushy, pushy mom. From my files comes a long
parade of witnesses.

Frankly, I think when my mother was a girl, she had wild
ideas about the things she would some day do. Then when
she couldn't do them, she kept driving me to make up for it.
It seems like I could never satisfy her. Sometimes I wonder if
I ever got over that.

You wouldn't believe the way my mother forced me to take
piano lessons and practice so long. Then one day I looked at
my stubby fingers and said, "How silly can you get; with hands
like mine, I should be a pianist?" Next came painting and a
bunch of other false efforts. It was a long time before I
understood that living out her failures wasn't my thing. And
did it ever feel good, when I decided that. It also seemed
like I wasn't quite so hungry anymore.

Mom would say, "Control yourself, Suzie." Then she would put me on a diet and get so mad when I couldn't stay on it. I finally figured this out. When I went on a diet, I was letting her control me. That's why nothing worked and sometimes I think I want to stay fat just to show I will not let her win. Isn't that silly?

It was like my mother's dreams were a parasite on me. I didn't realize this until I got older. But everything she did was designed to keep me in her power. It was awful.

My parents had some unbelievable ideas of all the great things I was going to do. It seems as if I resented this so much, I even set out to sabotage their dreams for me.

At our house it was like this. It seemed mother used food to seduce us into doing things her way. She would get furious if we deviated too much from her standards. For a long time this made me feel like a thing, not a person. As a child I didn't know how to handle it. So I think I ate to express myself or put me in a stupor or something.

Exactly how these testimonials apply will vary with the individual. Every fatty knows we eat for hidden reasons. Getting them all together takes a special measure of courage. Yet the painful process of facing all the facts is a must for the fat person's recovery. And fearless research on our mother's domination may be of special value.

CHECK QUESTION 8. *Is there a touch of hostility in our food habits?*
The mash-it-and-smash-it theme appears frequently in writings on obesity and overweight. This turns up often enough for us to pay it some attention.

Other psychological reactions include the release of hostilities through "taking it out" on food (smashing food between teeth).[1]

Oral dependence is only one aspect of the oral stage. The other aspect, oral sadism, is characterized by biting, chewing.[2]

We can observe this occasionally at restaurants or wherever people eat. These characters are called the "oral aggressives." And, according to the experts, there is a touch of it in all of us.

Personally, I have never consciously felt this way about foods. I tend to treat them kindly, as in tender loving care. But I do know the more I face my anger, the better.

Inner seething makes for hunger. This is why we need some place to ventilate our feelings wisely. The peace of God attained through self-analysis fills places in us which we may have been trying to stuff with food.

✻ ✻ ✻ ✻ ✻ ✻ ✻

PRAYER: Lord, I am grateful for my taste buds and the wonderful way foods differ. Sweets and sours and in-betweens. I like them all. And sometimes too much. Help me to appreciate without overloving. I cannot understand all of the criers far away in my childhood. But I know that with your help, I can determine right now to eat for you.

1. Arthur Dick, "Psychological Aspects of Obesity," *Medical Arts and Sciences,* third quarter, 1961, p. 97.
2. Joseph Masling and Lillie Rabie, "Obesity, Level of Aspiration, and Rorschach and Tat Measures of Oral Dependence," *Journal of Consulting Psychology,* 1967, 31:3, p. 233.

11
Mother's Food–
Comfort Me with Something Creamy

For everyone of us the oral syndrome differs. To each his own. What one eater does not like may be another person's "turn-on."

For me one of the certain tips I am feeling unloved is this—make it sweet, soft, rich, and give me another helping.

I know it could be a particular kind of taste buds. Nothing more, just body preference. But I've caught myself here too many times to believe it's all physiological. My loneliness goes better this way—comfort me with something creamy.

One psychiatrist says:

> The foods that best satisfy emotional needs are those that contain large amounts of refined sugar. This stems both from the influence of internal figures and from inherent qualities in the foods themselves.
> Many people experience a rapid improvement emotionally when they eat them, a result widely attributed to increase

in blood sugar. They may lead to addictive behavior in some people. So significant do the high-sugar-carbohydrate foods appear that my colleagues and I have come to call them "the pleasure foods." That is, foods that are used not primarily for nutrition, but for increase of pleasure. The hazard for the consumer of such foods is obesity or mal-nutrition or both together. Sorting these things out is not usually easy.[1]

Why did the Lord do us this way? If sweets made us thin and starches strong, life could be so enjoyable. But they won't, and we better face facts.

And we do well to remind ourselves here that our battle goes on forever. When we conquer one thing, another rises to tempt us. We master our craving for devil's food cake, but here comes a passion for chocolate ice cream, or vanilla, or twenty-six other flavors.

CHECK QUESTION 9 is especially for our favorite food: *Do we really need it for our hunger or do we want this for its taste?*
One beatitude from the Sermon on the Mount affirms, "Blessed are they which do hunger and thirst after righteousness for they shall be filled." A modern version puts it, "Blessed are those who hunger for the right thing." Which when applied to me calls for constant surveillance. Feeding our needs and nourishing our neuroses are not always the same thing. And sometimes it seems the whole world is set up to confuse us. Those food-related cues are everywhere.

Television, for instance. As if we didn't have enough problems, someone invented this hunger monster. Football, baseball, basketball, hockey, golf, racing—all alike. The same for the thrillers, westerns, documentaries, news, come-

---

1. Isabel Menzies, "Psychological Aspects of Eating," *Journal of Psychosomatic Research*, vol. 14, 1970, pp. 225–26.

dies, soap operas. Why do they go better with a direct route to the calories? I've even caught myself feeding my face when the taste was long gone.

The dictionary makes an interesting distinction between gourmand and gourmet.

A gourmand shovels it in because it's there and he still has room. He is a stuffer.

A gourmet is a connoisseur. He selects. He savors each bite. But taste and hunger are at his command.

Lord, help me to know the difference.

12
Mother Miscellany

From my personal correspondence comes this plaintive word of a fellow struggler. She is a mother herself now. Those who have had a touch of her agony will share her suffering. "I was dissolved into the greatest grief I have ever known, and with the grief came the knowledge that I had never had a place, an emotional place, in my mother's life. I had truly been an orphan from the time I was five. The desolation was total."

Say it one more time. We are never freed by hating our mother. So our praying here must include prayers for understanding tempered with mercy. Unless our mother was completely out of her mind, she did the best she could.

From various sources here are a few more questions worth checking.

CHECK QUESTION 10. *Were we ever denied foods as punishment?*

When I was a bad little boy, my parents used to spank me and send me to bed sometimes without my dinner. Would you believe that even today I can remember vividly how terrified I was. It was kind of like a double terror. I wondered if they would ever love me again. And I had this horrible feeling—what if some day I'd be so bad I'd never get to eat again? You can't imagine how awful that was. Recently I had an amazing insight. I realized that sometimes I eat today when I don't need it, just to be sure I'll have enough. (From the memories of a heavy friend.)

CHECK QUESTION 11. *Were we bribed with sweets?*

Do you suppose my yen for sweets could come from such a queer thing? My mother made a big deal out of candy and cake and all that stuff. What she did was to offer it to us as a reward when we had been especially good. Today, I think I reward myself in the same way. The odd thing is I often do it when I feel ashamed. It is like I am trying to prove to myself that I'm not all that bad. (A sharp young housewife.)

It helps me so much when I catch myself doing these crazy things, if I can stop long enough to ask, "Why are you stuffing with things you don't need?" When I bring myself up short with these questions, it really does the job. (From my correspondence file.)

CHECK QUESTION 12. *Were we ever narcotized with food, to shut us up, to get us out of the way?*
Is there a mother alive who hasn't done it some time? Give him a bottle . . . cracker . . . cookie . . . ice cream raisins . . . lollypop . . . doughnut . . . banana . . . anything. . . . If you'll just be quiet a little while.
How can this possibly be affecting us today? One contender for normal contours describes it well:

Our parents were both lawyers and very successful. We were raised by a nurse, a great cook, and she loved us. I'm sure the folks did too. Only I worried a lot about it. Even

77

when they weren't working, they spent so much time at the club. "Business," they said. They would give us all these nice things, so many in fact, I think it made me suspicious. I got the feeling that all those toys and beautiful presents and rich food were to get us out of their way. For a long time I think I ate to fill a kind of chronic emptiness.

CHECK QUESTION 13. *Did our mother overemphasize how much we owed her?*
Every person in his right mind wants to do right by his parents. We are repelled by any obvious neglect of these responsibilities. But there are homes which overplay this theme. If ours was one of these, it may have produced in us a false sense of responsibility. Anyone brought up with such a pseudodebt will understand.

If there is a gnawing sense of obligation in our subconscious, it needs firm handling.

I remember one time at a friend's birthday party, I heard her parents tell her, "Betty Jean, we are so glad we have you." That was a beautiful new note to me. At our house it was always the other way around. I'm not sure how this affects my eating, but I think it does. It seems like I want to be overly nice to me because I am trying so hard to appreciate myself.

* * * * * * *

SUMMARY: There is an interesting term used often by psychiatrists to describe our family memories. They call it "the internal society."

The internal society is a particularly significant influence in determining behavior about food and eating. . . . The baby's feeling about the feeding mother and what she does or does not do for him are intense and extreme. Food given by a loving and skilled mother helps the baby to feel safe, sane

78

and well rooted in life. . . . I am talking of the mother as the baby takes her in and experiences her as an *internal* mother, not the mother as she really is. The baby's feeling can turn a good, real mother into an experienced bad one and vice versa. . . . One may truly say that people eat in the context of the internal society. These primitive causal connections remain with us as we grow up.[1]

PRAYER: Lord, I am grateful for every good thing my mother gave me. Thank you. Teach me to draw back the dark curtain of the negatives. Help me to examine them honestly for every effect they may have on me today. I would be forgiving of the bad that I might be appreciative of the good. *Amen.*

---

1. Isabel Menzies, "Psychological Aspects of Eating," *Journal of Psychosomatic Medicine,* vol. 1, 1970, pp. 223–27.

13
And Then There Was Dad

Psychiatrists do not say much about the fat person's father relationships. Perhaps it is because our food recall is mostly on the maternal side. Yet there are enough witnesses from the other direction to make it worth our study. I once did some research among heavies I have known. I asked them to surface their father feelings. Here's what they had to say:

My old man was kind of a nonentity. I always thought of him as a thing. Mom wore the pants, and he let her.

Rigid was the word for mine. He was always right about everything. Super religious. Judgmental. It was pretty grim for all of us.

My dad was a huge success in almost every way. He drove himself and my mother and me.

When I realized I could never reach his expectations, I think I began to eat to prove something. If I couldn't be the best, at least I'd be the biggest.

Mine was something like that too. He was always raising hell about my being overweight. Could it be that I stayed fat just because I didn't want him to be all that smart about everything?

Poppa was huge and I was crazy about him. So I guess for a long time I was trying to be like him.

My father was gone a lot. And when he was home, he seemed so aloof. I had a friend whose daddy was the greatest. I remember asking myself, "How come mine can't be my friend like that?"

I got the best grades of everybody in my class, and my father was so proud of me. But then I caught on. He really wasn't as interested in me as he was in my grades. It seemed like I was just an extension of his ego.

Ours was very strict in every way, including what we ate. Only he didn't have any idea about healthy foods. Real often, when he came home from work, he would bring a sackful of rich things from the bakery. When he died, I missed his firmness. I finally figured out that I ate too much heavy stuff to recapture the feelings I got from his bakery goods. It was like they would somehow bring back his caring and strictness.

One further child-father consideration may be affecting our religious responses. If we were taught to pray, "Our Father, who art in heaven"; if we attended Sunday school regularly; if the language of our home was in a religious vernacular—we might need some inner research here. Unpleasant father relationships could be affecting our feeling for God!

Children, unable to contrast, tend to compare. If the paternal experience was not good, feeling for deity may be the same. Yet there is no percentage in beating any memory to death.

So wherever our father-mother recall takes a down trend, these are the steps for recovery:

1. I must conduct an honest research and surface the truth.

2. I must face the facts and apply them to my present eating habits.

3. Since resentment produces hunger, and anger stimulates appetite, I must forgive.

4. For all of my negative yesterdays, and every relationship today, there is only one antidote: I must try to love others as God loves me.

14
Reality Therapy

"This one thing I do, forgetting those things which are behind, and reaching forth unto those things which are before, I press toward the mark" (Phil. 3:13–14).

Navel-gazing is the current term for excessive retrospect. And Paul was against it. He refers us often to his ugly past. But his theme seems to be: Wherever negative memories bless you, use them. Then lay them aside and move on."

Reality Therapy is a fresh breeze on the psychiatric scene. Yet it is really no new thing. In Philippians 3:13-14, Paul sounds the same note—the time finally comes when we have done enough digging. Tomorrow matters more than yesterday.

No one can tell where the fine line is for each of us. We must work this out on our own. But here are some of my clues for times when I'm overdoing the backward look:

1. When my memories have more resentment than thanksgiving. Almost every person who affected me badly blessed me also in another way.

2. When I begin to feel sorry for myself. Everyone I know has had some unfortunate experiences. I have no right to expect exemption from trouble.

3. When I'm failing to change now what can be changed by me. To let the unchangeable things of my past dominate me has to be evil. It cripples me. It hinders the plan of God.

All these things come through clearly as I ponder Reality Therapy. And some of their emphasis I need—"Quit blaming others. The past is over and gone. You can do nothing about it now." But for most of us fatties it's an oversimplification. There are some things we can do about our yesterdays.

Still, the Reality Therapists are right about this: Looking back is unhealthy when we should be moving forward.

So we can be grateful for every productive insight. And we can be glad for the Reality Therapists when they call us to move on.

III

I Am Thankful

Introduction

The Bible is never explicit about Paul's "thorn in the flesh."

Some scholars say it was epilepsy. That would be embarrassing for a public speaker. Others opt for poor eyesight. For a teacher like Paul this would be especially difficult. Another school of thought believes he was a hunchback. But nobody knows for sure. Always there is a fuzziness here. Perhaps God knew it would be best this way.

Biblical books are not arranged by the order in which they were written. So when we rearrange them by their dates, we see some new things.

While I was losing one hundred twenty pounds, many verses from Paul spoke loud and clear to me. Then I began to study his letters in the order of their writing. Now I came to a fresh insight. Whatever his problem, as he grew older, he seemed to have a better grip on it. And every retake brought me to the same conclusion: this man was my fellow struggler.

So my guess is that he had a weight problem. I think he might have been a fatty just like us.

And you, too, will sing
when you have at last recognized
and see the promises of God where
you saw only torment.[1]

1

When the Bad Things Turn to Good

*"And lest I should be exalted above measure . . . there
was given to me a thorn in the flesh, . . . For this thing
I besought the Lord thrice, that it might depart from me.
And he said unto me, My grace is sufficient for thee: for
my strength is made perfect in weakness. Most gladly
therefore will I rather glory in my infirmities"* (2 Cor. 12:
7–9).

Some fascinating studies are under way in medical science.
One is reported in Hans Selye's book *The Stress of Life*.[2] This
eminent doctor has given his talents to an unusual research.
It is a known fact that man is equipped with innate healing
qualities. Physicians count on these to help the patient recover.

"What," asks Dr. Selye, "is the frame of mind most in-

---

1. Louis Evely, *The Word of God* (New York: Herder & Herder, 1967), p. 16.
2. Hans Selye, *The Stress of Life* (New York: McGraw Hill, 1956).

ducive to returning health? Which attitudes stimulate a quick response?" After years of diligent searching, he came to this one word answer: *Thanksgiving*.

I needed that. I find myself too often scolding God. So do most of my fat friends. Naturally, we don't do this consciously. But in our unawareness there may be some secret resentment. Why should I have a problem like this? Other people can eat and eat and eat. I know. For thirty years I've been watching one.

You can hardly believe the date bread she makes . . . the pecan rolls . . . her Danish gravies . . . prune coffee cake . . . turkey dressing . . . her blueberry cheese concoctions.

They drive me out of my mind. And sometimes they make me furious. Especially, they do when she can sample them with hardly a thought for her waistline. And me? Every calorie settles down for a long stay. (This may be highly unscientific, but I think of calories as two kinds, the "waltzers" and the "heavies.")

So now I'm supposed to be thankful. And it's not always easy. But I know the Apostle is right. This grudge against God is a very big negative.

One of the major landmarks in my recovery came right here. If Paul could glory in his infirmities, I could glory in mine. Whatever his thorn in the flesh, the handle was thanksgiving. He quit carping and I would. When I surrendered my resentment, a wonderful thing happened. My problem wasn't all problem now. In it there was also a blessing.

****

SCRIPTURES FOR THE DAY: "It is good for me that I have been afflicted; that I might learn thy statutes" (Ps. 119:71).

"Discipline, no doubt, is never pleasant; at the time it

seems painful, but in the end it yields for those who have been trained by it the peaceful harvest of an honest life" (Heb. 12:13, NEB).

"My son, despise not the chastening of the Lord; neither be weary of his correction: For whom the Lord loveth he correcteth; even as a father the son in whom he delighteth" (Prov. 3:11).

2
The Shape We're In, Talks!

"But I pommel my body and subdue it, lest after preaching to others, I myself should be disqualified" (2 Cor. 9:27, RSV).

Kierkegaard was over my head. Most of the Danish philosopher's stuff went much too deep for me. But I did well in our seminary course on the famous theologian. The reason was a little book of his parables. I found it hidden back in the library stacks, apparently long forgotten. These little tales I could easily remember. So whenever we came to an examination, I quoted liberally from the Kierkegaard stories. This brought me a passing grade, plus some lessons I have not forgotten.

One of these is his parable of the fat parson. Kierkegaard liked to go on a Sunday evening to hear other preachers. He called it filling his basket. This particular night, he made his way to a small country church. The huge pastor came out from behind the pulpit and draped his avoirdupois over the chancel railing. Then folding his hands sanctimoniously on his fat belly, he began, "Brothers and sisters, tonight I want to talk to you on the text, 'If any man would come after me, let him deny himself.'"

To which Kierkegaard muses, "The pity was nobody laughed."

You may not like it, and I don't, but the shape we are in *talks*. So much is written about our problem that we can find no place to hide. Even the casual reader knows that overpadding is partly psychological. We cancel our right to say some things by lugging too much poundage.

Paul doesn't specify what he means by pommeling his body. But he is specific about this possibility: Words are not enough. Sometimes how we look cancels what we say.

Most of us fatties know every camouflage. Dresses without belts . . . shirts hanging over our waistlines . . . pleated pants . . . baggy sweaters . . . loose coats. Yet who are we kidding really? No one. Fat with any kind of cover up is still fat.

But there is another side to the verse for today. If we can master our problem, that too is visible. Obesity subdued and overweight brought to submission is sure to inspire. Seeing us, some fellow struggler under his burden may take heart. And God knows one hundred million heavies need every kind of encouragement.

* * * * * * *

FOR PONDERING: "O God, thou knowest my foolishness; and my sins are not hid from thee" (Ps. 69:5).

There is another temptation, which
is very common; when people
begin to have pleasure in the fruit of
prayer, they will have everybody
else to be very spiritual also.
Now to desire this is not wrong, but to
try to bring it about may not be
right, except with great discretion and
with much reserve, without any
appearance of teaching.[1]

3
The Pushy, Pushy Me

*"The man who will eat anything must not look down on the
man who abstains from some things, and the man who abstains from them must not criticize the one who does not"*
(Rom. 14:3, Goodspeed).

Comes now another fact which needs guarding: Those
of us who are overweight tend to be judgmental. Especially after we have lost a few pounds, we mount the pulpit
to convert the whole fat world.

Why? Maybe we feel so good we'd like our chubby
friends to feel good also. Perhaps since we have been loaded
down so long, we develop a zeal to liberate society. There
could be other positive reasons. But some of our pushiness
is not from pure motives. Our desire to help could be nothing more than inverted self-praise.

Paul must have known this problem. But as the years pass
he reveals a changing attitude. His earlier works are heavy
with the spirit of *you* sinners. Later, he quits judging others
and calls *himself* chief of the bad guys.

1. Jean Pierre DeCaussade, *On Prayer,* p. 221.

When we are honest, this same process will be taking place in us. We should find ourselves turning away from the windows through which we study the faults of others. If we are authentic, we will be at the mirror observing our own errors.

Most of us have enough negatives inside to keep us busy. Cornering these and surrendering them is a full-time job.

At our best we should be ready to help anyone who comes to us. But until they do, Paul's word is our warning. Abstainer and eater alike are not on trial before us. Our business is to love all and be true to our own commitment.

****

PRAYER: Lord, help me not to be a bore. When I am preachy, nudge me. When I am boasting, stop me. When I recite how I did it, check me. Help me to remember that the other fellow is more interested in himself than in me. Whenever I am trying to overconvert the world, tell it to me straight. *Amen.*

4
Big Brother Is Watching

"For a man's ways are before the eyes of the Lord, and he watches all his paths" (Prov. 5:21, RSV).

Including the path to the refrigerator, the bakery, and the malt shop.

There is something repugnant in the big-brother-is-watching theme. It is frequently used as a warning against too much governmental scrutiny. Limitless wiretapping makes us angry, and it should. Freedom is one of our most precious possessions.

The fatty knows what it means to be watched and watched. At every church dinner there is one self-appointed policeman. Why does she sit across from me? Why does she have such a loud voice? Why does she wait for an audience to shout observations on my food choice? And when I sit down for a surreptitious piece of pie à la mode, same thing.

Why does the waitress have such big eyes? The candy store in the shopping mall lures me. It draws me in. Chocolates, gum drops, and all those things I like so much. But when I'm inside I find another thing. These places seem to have eyes in the corners. Judging eyes. Condemning.

Blessed is the fatty who has a friend to help him handle his problem. Yet even when we invite someone's surveillance, we may catch ourselves playing funny little games. We try to outmaneuver our helpers. We think if they don't catch us, it won't make us fat. Silly? Sure. But these odd little quirks are all part of our battle.

Still, what the wise man of Proverbs says is really comforting. When we understand our God is not a big bad policeman, things change. When we know he watches all our paths because he cares for us, we will be grateful.

Eighteen times the Bible refers to "the eyes of the Lord." Some of these give strong warnings about doing what is right. But when we come at them positively, most of them say a very nice thing.

"The eyes of the Lord are in every place" (Prov. 15:3); "The eyes of the Lord run to and fro" (2 Chron. 16:9); "The eyes of the Lord range through the whole earth" (Zech. 4:10, RSV); "The eyes of the Lord are upon the righteous" (Ps. 34:15, 2 Pet. 3:12).

Add to these the references to God's "watch," his "seeing," "looking" and we come to an awesome realization. There is no hiding place.

When we are behaving ourselves, this is a beautiful truth: Our God is everywhere, sees everything, knows all. And whether we like it or not depends on us. He watches our paths, he cares what we eat, because he loves us.

We can be thankful for this too.

✳ ✳ ✳ ✳ ✳ ✳ ✳

"Whatever you do, whether you eat or drink, do all to the glory of God" (1 Cor. 10:31, RSV).

96

5
Ten Must Attitudes for Right Eating

This is not a book about diets. It isn't about foods and their make-up. We need to be as scientific and intelligent as possible. Carbohydrates, proteins, fats, sugars, minerals, vitamins, caloric content, all these are important. Yet we are only the nearest magazine away from another article on helps for the heavy. (Question: Why do the editors place these things between all those elegant pictures—savory dishes, exotic desserts, snacks to drive us out of our mind?)

So with a deluge of diets and sundry writings on foods, nobody needs more from me. But I would like to share with you what I call "My Ten Must Attitudes for Right Eating."

1. I must educate myself in food values, calorie contents, health-giving nutriments.

2. I must train myself to eat slowly and *taste* each bite. Taste is not bad unless I overdo it. Where I formerly stuffed on quantity, I must learn to appreciate quality.

97

3. Second helpings must be checked against this question: Do I *need* it or do I merely *want* it? I have come to this conclusion: With me it takes a while for my stomach to send a message to my brain. In other words, I may be physically full but my head doesn't know it. So, sometimes if I wait, I realize I don't need it.

4. I must learn to live on the edge of hunger. There is no way to retain my shape and have all I want. And this is for sure, I can never get fat on what I don't eat.

5. I must be continually evaluating what I eat. Some foods have more staying power than others. And some of the best tasters do me the least good.

6. I must make friends with this hard fact: If it's sweet, it's probably not for me. (Unless I'm sure the sweetener is artificial.)

7. I must be alert to constant food danger. At home, in public places, everywhere, I am subject to temptation.

8. I must be glad that others can eat freely. I will not punish myself nor the rest of the world with my problem.

9. I must put my commitment ahead of pressures from other people. I will try to be gracious, but I must be firm. (For me the most effective way to say no is to tell it like it is. Most people understand when I say, "I'm a foodaholic. It looks delicious, but if you don't mind, I'll enjoy the company while you eat.")

10. Any diet, fast or semifast, must be medically approved.

✿✿✿✿✿✿✿

PRAYER BEFORE MEALTIME: Thank you, Lord, for all these products of your goodness. Who but a wise Creator would think to make beans green, milk white, carrots orange, strawberries red? Who blesses my life with smells? Who gives me the money to buy this food? And a mind to discern what's right for me? Teach me to eat with wisdom and a glad heart. *Amen.*

Though it is a bitter pill to
swallow for a patient who has hoped
for a golden era, he has to learn . . .
potentiality for his special
malfunctioning always remains
with him.[1]

6
The Odyssey of a Fat Man Who Lost a Ton

"*I die daily*" (1 Cor. 15:31).

Me too, Paul.

Watching my weight is a drag some days. Will I never be liberated? Can I ever eat anything, everything, and all I want of it?

To which comes the same monotonous answer: "No! This is forever." Some of the inner raging may never cease. At least with me it hasn't for twenty years.

This is the story of my life, the odyssey of a fat man who lost a ton. Sometimes I'm up. Sometimes I'm down. You won't believe it if you've never been there. But adding them all together, two thousand pounds over the years may be conservative.

My range is fifteen pounds up and down. Which Yo-Yo is very well known to most of my heavy friends. But though the scale may vary, there is never a change in this truth. We will always be fat prone. And we are forever in need of commitment.

---

1. Andras Angyal, *Neurosis and Treatment* (New York: John Wiley and Sons, 1965), p. 260.

The smart college boy said an interesting thing. "The trouble with religion is that it's so darn daily." Right. That is also what makes it beautiful, and the beauty comes when we approach each day with thanksgiving.

One of the giant steps forward is to lay away forever the futile hope of unlimited quantities. We haven't arrived at the threshold of victory until we accept this fact. Indiscriminate eating is not for us ever.

One of the fat person's tendencies is to live in fantasy. Among our favorites is to imagine a distant day when *we* will be making the rules. Then everything will be so nice for us. But always and for all times these are siren voices to which we must not listen. The ones for us are those with the hard sounds: "You will never be that free. Your problem is forever and daily."

AWESOME THOUGHT: What if judgment for us was God asking how we had used our problem. Great liberating concept here. He knows what we need better than we do. It doesn't matter whether we like it. What matters is whether God likes it for us.

****

THOUGHT FOR MEDITATION: "Must we always struggle, never winning, never reaching the goal line? The answer is an unqualified yes. The struggle here never ends, but with every step of the earthly pilgrimage there is a new sense of inner peace and quiet, the growing sense of a Presence working with and within us." [2]

2. Cecil Osborne, *The Art of Understanding Yourself* (Grand Rapids: Zondervan Publishing House, 1967), p. 82.

No prayer will be answered so long
as we are cherishing feelings of
resentment. . . . still less can we expect
an answer if we are secretly rebelling
against the will of God. . . .
if we are refusing to accept the
circumstances in which we have been
placed and are constantly dreaming
of what we could do "if things
were different" our prayers will not be
answered. . . . God cannot do
anything for us while we are in this
state of mind.[1]

7

Today I Don't Like You, Lord

*"Wherefore hidest thou thy face, and forgettest our afflic-
tion and our oppression?"* (Ps. 44:24).

When I was in seminary our professor of psychiatry taught
us a good thing. He said that to like totally we must surface our dislikes completely. Unless we do this, he con-
tended, the positive will never be more than semi. Of
course, he went on to explain, this must be carefully
handled. Some people can stand yelling and screaming.
They respond to it without cratering. But for most of us it
goes better another way. We can learn to express our hostility thoroughly but gently.

Usually, for the fatty, this kind of honesty is something
new. Even with all our pounds we develop quick feet for
side-stepping. As one overweight girl puts it, "If it's unpleasant, I won't face it. And as long as I can remember,
I've been the world's best pretender. I pretend it didn't

1. Olive Wyon, *Prayer* (London: Collins Clear-Type Press, Fontana paperback, 1962), p. 91.

happen. I pretend it isn't so. I pretend it's going away. To show you how hopeless I am, when you tell me some day I'll have to face it—I even pretend I'm not hearing you."

We know what she means. The average fat person has a history of considerable deceit in relationships.

The origin of this expertise may be long gone. Psychiatrists say it goes far back, maybe to infancy. It might have begun out of necessity, for self-protection, to preserve our ego. But here is one place where the road back is not as important as the road forward. And that road for me began in a new relationship with God.

One day in my study I came on this truth which I had overlooked. The great men of Scripture didn't always like God. *And they told him so.* Jeremiah, Habakkuk, Job, the psalmist, plus many others voiced their complaints openly. Mildly sometimes. Sometimes not so mildly. And sometimes vociferously. They said it loud and clear—"Today I don't like you, Lord. And here's why: You're picking on me. Can't you hear my crying? Why aren't you listening? I think you're hiding. Have you forgotten how it hurts?"

Maybe this is one reason they cared so much. For their great battles they needed a total relationship. The clear voice of God's support called for a clear track between them. The experts at prayer, both ancient and modern, are increasingly honest.

Mature relationships with people are not all sweetness and light. We have done a great thing for ourselves when we learn the art of being completely open. There are acceptable ways to express anger. And we must train ourselves carefully. Hidden rage may gradually build up inside like a pressure cooker. Leaving our fury unsettled, we might literally eat until it hurts. And the greatest hurt may be the long-range damage to both body and conscience.

TRUTH: The purest honesty is honesty with God.

Blessed is he who can totally like God because he has totally surfaced his dislikes.

It has been known for a long
time that when parents are fat,
children are more likely to be fat. But
no one knew whether this was
hereditary or whether it was because
families who eat together tend to
grow fat together. Now it can be said
with certainty that genetic factors
do *play a part*. . . . the studies
of heredity show that obesity as such, is
not hereditary but that the type of
body build is, plus a predisposition to
obesity. What can a doctor do
to give you different genes and
chromosomes so that your body build
and predisposition to obesity will
be changed? Nothing. Yet, you
can prevent a predisposition
from becoming a reality but you have
to struggle for what the normal
person takes for granted.[1]

8

Nature or Too Much Nurture

*"Look to the rock from which you were hewn, and to the
quarry from which you were digged"* (Isa. 51:1, RSV).

As I studied in medical libraries, I came often on certain
quotations which reappeared like old friends. One of these
is from an unknown author. He must have been a nice kind
of wag to know. "The way to prevent obesity," he says, "is to
shop around for parents of slender build six months before
you're born."

1. S. D. Kaplan, Ph.D., "Obesity and the Emotions," *Nebraska State Medical
Journal*, February 1966, pp. 41–42.

The Bible reminds us frequently that we can profit from a backward look. Both New Testament and Old call us to turn around occasionally for our own good. The prophets especially trumpet this note. Sometimes their appeal was to nations, but any serious reader senses another truth. Nations are made of people, and warnings are only effective when applied personally.

Isaiah was a champion of individual application. Always the call of God for him went beyond people to the person. But in a very real sense, no person is a pure individual. We have all been shaped by others. And right here is one of our major temptations.

High on the fat man's list of alibis is, "It runs in my family." "All our folks are heavy." "My mother and father were both plump." (Brothers, sisters, cousins, aunts, uncles, grandpas, grandmas do as well.)

QUESTION: How authentic are these alibis?

ANSWER: Nobody knows for sure.

There is considerable disagreement here. Some say we can practically disregard our heritage. Others contend it makes a mighty difference. After putting it all together, I have come to these conclusions for me:

1. Overweight and obesity may not be inherited, but tendencies in these directions are. Body types vary with pedigrees. Some physical systems tend to use food fast. Some, like mine, are ultraeconomical. They retain calories which others burn quickly.

2. Eating habits are often inherited, not from ancient history, but from the family table. This is not heredity in its purest sense. But in practical application, it is every bit as significant. The same goes for attitudes toward food. It is especially important to check what food meant to us as we were growing up. Are we eating for meanings which no

longer exist? For the obese and overweight, heritage of our own making needs careful scrutiny.

3. Our physical size and tendencies aren't all we inherit. Some mental and emotional characteristics also come down ancestral roads. The high-tempered father, overbearing mother, weaknesses, strengths—all parental stances are important. This is why counselors making up case histories inquire into our background.

Any combination of emotional characteristics in our forbears could stamp us for good or for bad.

So, what does all this mean?

One sure meaning is that *attitudes toward our history are more important than the history*. It does no good to pine over the sleek neighbor. We never lose weight by coveting the other person's physical make-up. Shape and symmetry, to a certain extent, may be outside our influence. But what's inside today is our own doing.

As we "look to the rock from which we were hewn, and to the quarry from which we were digged," we can sing a glad song for this thought: Before our family heritage, back of the psychological molding, we come from God.

****

PRAYER: Heavenly Father, I am glad to be alive. I pray for the courage to face my past intelligently. Help me to understand my shape and my shaping. Where I can never be different, teach me acceptance. Where others influenced me in the negative, make me merciful. Where you and I together can rework me, show me my part. Thank you for giving me life in any form. *Amen.*

Active exercise as a means to
lose weight is of no value. To lose one
pound a person would have to walk
at fast pace without stopping
for a distance of thirty-three miles.[1]

OR

The entire condition of the patient,
both mental and physical, is
improved by exercise. Not only does
exercise utilize energy and
thereby favor reduction of weight,
but it also prevents atrophy of
muscles and other important tissues. It
preserves and strengthens many
vital functions. . . . for instance,
the activity of the heart, the liver,
and the kidneys.[2]

9

Exercise, Exercise,
I Must Do My Exercise

"Physical exercise has some value" (1 Tim. 4:8, TEV).

There are experts who say exercise is all important. Others give it a zero. From the wide range of opinions, we can take our choice. Paul's word *some* may be where it is.

After twenty years of experimentation, I have come to these conclusions.

1. Whatever the exercise, the key word is *steady*.

It works best if I develop a modest program on a regular basis. Every day is better than three times weekly. Any less is practically useless.

---

1. S. William Kalb, M.D., "The Management of Obesity," *Journal of the Medical Society of N.J.*, September 1958.
2. Thomas Hodge McGavack, M.D., "Treatment of Uncomplicated Obesity," *The Medical Clinics of N.A.*, November 1961.

2. *Reducing equipment is not the answer.*

I've bought them all. Like the majority of my fat friends, I am a first-class sucker for the admakers. But for me, the more they promise to take it off without effort, the more I should flee from their frenzy. With exercise, if it doesn't call for exertion, it's a waste of my money and emotional hope.

3. *The best exercise is something I enjoy.*

If I go to it grudgingly, it won't last. The catch is that it may take up to thirty days to tell whether I enjoy it. Or to come at it from the other side, at first I might not enjoy anything. Most of us who have been obese and overweight tend to dislike all exercise. We may even hate it. We have been inactive too long.

Some psychiatrists contend our dislike of exercise is related to a dislike of the body. We rebel, they say, because we don't like our present size and shape. Since we don't like it, why knock ourselves out to improve it? But this is a fact: The more fun I can make it, the longer I'll stay with it.

4. *It's good for me if it makes me feel good all over.*

One doctor, whose opinion I respect, tells me the secret is what he calls "exergesis." That has something to do with energy going out. I can't explain it adequately, but it comes through to me with this important meaning: The only way to get new energy is to use old energy. Like many things, we must use it to replace it. As we release the tired old stuff, fresh supplies move in.

5. *My exercise goes better with thanksgiving.*

When I consider my years of overfeeding, as I ponder the destruction I have escaped, remembering the many I know who cannot move as I move, I am overcome with gratitude.

Why should I be so fortunate? Considering my treatment of me, only God's goodness makes my exercise possible.

6. *Exercise is never a substitute for right eating.*

You say a good thing, Paul, for me. "Physical exercise has *some* value." One of my funny fat friends paraphrases Omar Khayyám, "A piece of lettuce, exercise, and thou." Total program!

Perhaps one day scientists
will discover that some glandular change
is brought on by prayer or
meditation.[1]

10

Thanks Too for the Unknown

"Let God transform you inwardly" (Rom. 12:2, TEV).

I don't know as much about bodies as the doctors do. But
I have been over an arduous road inside this one body. And
I believe what the man says about "perhaps one day
scientists will discover some glandular change is brought
on by prayer or meditation." Except "perhaps one day" has
the feel of the real to me. As I pray for insight, I sense
my body making some changes for the good inside.

Psyche (mind), *soma* (body) can have real meaning for
the obese and overweight. Things under the surface may be
keeping us fat. Coming to it from the negative side, we
see the destruction of our buried feelings. Repressed hostility. Envy. Unsurfaced guilt. Hatred. All their ilk. Nobody
knows for sure the damage they do. We may say, "I'll forget
it," but the question is, "Does it forget us?" Doctors tell
us it might not. Some claim even our size can be affected by
our hidden thoughts.

1. Walter Starcke, *The Ultimate Revolution* (New York: Harper & Row, 1969),
p. 124.

The fears and rebellions and apprehensions and hatreds of childhood are not merely psychological experiences. They help to determine the ratio and distribution of materials from which the body is built. And from this, the actual physical structure is directly affected.[2]

Such a mysterious process remains an enigma. But there are enough who sound this note that I do well to listen. And I better listen to Paul too. Here and in countless other places, he adds to the medic's thesis. And his added note is that I can't do it alone. One translator rewrites Romans 12:2, "Let God remold your minds from within" (Phillips).

PRAYER: Lord, it says in the Book that I am fearfully and wonderfully wrought. I accept that. I have felt my body yield as my mind surrendered to your will. I want to do "what is good, and pleasing and perfect" for you and for me. Transform me inwardly. Remold me. Shape me. Thank you. *Amen.*

---

2. James Tucker Fisher, *A Few Buttons Missing* (Philadelphia: J. B. Lippincott, 1951), p. 120.

11
Signs of Progress

Hypnotism is another technique with a record of some success in weight loss. Maybe for other people, but not for me. I've tried this and it's one more negative. Experts admit it won't work with certain types. I'm one.

It's probably my fault because I can't picture food in the negative. "All of those things that make you fat—think of them now as revolting. Conjure up some horrible image and attach it to the devil's food cake. Burning rubber. The smell of wet feathers. Can't you think something repulsive and connect it with all those calories?" I tried. Honestly. Hard. Yet it always came out the same way. Fats, sweets, desserts, rich foods. Beautiful! In fact, the harder I tried to make them horrid, the more they turned out scrumptious. So another dead end to a high hope.

Still, given enough time, I believe in the power of mind over body. With me the changes came slowly. And I have certain signs of progress I keep going back to. These are questions I put to myself.

1. Over an extended period, am I able to hold my weight within a limited range? As my scale moves toward my self-imposed ceiling, can I blow the whistle on me?

2. When I know I must go on a diet, do I face it calmly? Does the threat of a spartan regime panic me less than the last time?

3. Am I becoming easier to live with? Do I project my problem as much as I once did? Punish others less? Care more for their feelings?

4. Am I gaining a more practical view of my own importance? Is my drive to be center stage subsiding? Am I increasingly able to feel the needs and the worth of other people?

5. Is my hostility fuse growing longer? Are the things which once made me fly off the handle becoming more manageable? Rejection, criticism, plain old ugliness from others, can I meet these with more mercy?

6. Does self-analysis frighten me less? Am I able to go down deeper now? Can I stay down longer and come up with more as I research inside me?

7. Am I discovering more of the real me? Doing more things because I want to? Not for acclaim or some one else's approval, but mine? The self I was meant to be, is it coming alive?

8. Can I give up my dreams of a cure and settle for a solution?

9. The great indicator I'm getting better: Do I understand more clearly what God wants me to be? Am I increasingly willing to live his way?

* * * * * * *

PRAYER: Thank you Lord for every small sign. *Amen.*

12
And Many More Things
from the Apostle

At this point in our study we have used numerous verses from writings of Paul. All of these have meant something to me on my pilgrimage to better proportions.

My theory that his thorn in the flesh may have been obesity came through gradually. As I studied the Bible for help in my struggle, I focused on words like *body, appetite, eating, food, physical*. Along with these, I turned to such terms as *habit, self-control, dedication, desire*. Paul used them frequently.

The Book speaks to each of us personally. For this reason what we dig out ourselves is likely to be especially helpful. In addition to the writings already cited, here are more references from Paul which have helped me along the way.

"Each of you should learn to master his own body" (1 Thess. 4:4, The Epistles of Paul, Conybeare).

"I mean this: if you are guided by the Spirit you will not

fulfil the desires of your lower nature. Those who belong to Christ Jesus have crucified the lower nature with its passions and desires. If the Spirit is the source of our life, let the Spirit also direct our course. So let us never tire of doing good, for if we do not slacken our efforts we shall in due time reap our harvest" (Gal. 5:16, 24–25, 6:9, NEB).

"God keeps his promise, and he will not allow you to be tempted beyond your power to resist" (1 Cor. 10:13, TEV).

"Let him that thinketh he standeth take heed lest he fall" (1 Cor. 10:12).

"Do not, for the sake of food, be tearing down God's work" (Rom. 14:20, The Centenary Translation: The New Testament in Modern English).

"People who are controlled by the physical think of what is physical" (Rom. 8:5, Goodspeed).

"I appeal to you, therefore, brothers, by this mercy of God, to offer your bodies in a living sacrifice that will be holy and acceptable to God" (Rom. 12:1, Goodspeed).

"They let their good food and other blessings trap them into believing that all was well between themselves and God" (Rom. 11:9, The Living Bible).

"He is a fortunate man who has no misgivings about what he allows himself to eat. But if anyone has doubts about eating and then eats, that condemns him at once" (Rom. 14:22–23, Moffatt).

"For, as I have often told you, and now tell you with tears in my eyes, there are many whose way of life makes them enemies of the cross of Christ. They are heading for destruction, appetite is their god, and they glory in their shame" (Phil. 3:18–19, NEB).

"Under Christ's control the whole body is nourished and held together by its joints and ligaments, and grows as God wants it to grow" (Col. 2:19, TEV).

IV

I Begin Again

1
That Knock on the Back Door

"But now that you have come to know God, . . . how can you turn back again . . . ?" (Gal. 4:9, RSV).

Most of us heavies have been down this road ten thousand times: We turned our problem over to God. We *really* did. We meant every word of our surrender. But then one day we went knocking on his back door to ask for its return.

And he gave it to us.

The amazing courtesy of God is beautiful. Extra beautiful. Wonderful, wonderful liberty. But with a problem like ours, his very goodness exposes us to danger. He never forces us, never keeps us waiting. Whenever we wish to renege on our surrender, God treats us with dignity. Temporary? Permanent? It's our decision.

I always tremble a bit when I hear someone say, "I'm a Christian." Nothing the matter with that if it means, "I'm working at it with God's help." But for us this "working at it" must be the life style.

Three times daily we are faced with the test. Or, to be

exact, it's three dozen times or three hundred. Every time we pass the refrigerator, the bakery, the vending machine, there's that test again.

Sometimes it would be so much easier if the Lord set our plate and limited the selections. This much to eat, and only this. That's it for today. No more. Salads. Juices. Vegetables. Meats. You've had it. Now run along and be good. But always and forever he gives us this one thing more: Freedom to do it our way or his.

"How can you turn back again?" One reason is that our Creator made us for living on two levels. Below our awareness there is another life going on. And down under we do no small part of our business. Being the way God made us, the threat is forever there. Two minds—awareness, unawareness. Two motions—forward, backward.

So what is the answer? What can we do with this double trouble?

We can begin right here with a double surrender. We can thank God for God. Because he is like he is, we can knock on his door again. And he will welcome us. Any time.

For the obese and overweight this is the Good News.

* * * * * * *

PRAYER: Today, Lord, I make a two-way surrender. Both parts of me. Here at the front of my mind, there in the back rooms, come in! Have your way all the way. When I turn from my good intentions, reclaim me. Thank you for another chance, and ten thousand. *Amen.*

2
He Runs to Meet Us

"While he was still a long way off, his father saw him, and his heart went out to him" (Luke 15:20, NEB).

It was a wise little girl who said, "Jesus is the best photograph God ever had took." She says it well for us fatties. Most of us need nothing so bad as a clear concept of Deity. It is crucial that we understand God's amazing grace.

This concept is imperative for one deadly reason. Say it again: All God's overblown sons and daughters have grandiose ideas. We can't bear failure. Instead of accepting our weakness, we spin off into self-incrimination. Which has the same inevitable effect if we don't correct it. Bring on the food. And all the while the Father waits.

He waits for us to measure our repeated failures against his mercy. And any slight move from us in his direction brings him running. That's what it says in Luke 15, the story of the Prodigal Son. If by some misfortune we had to discard all but one chapter of the Bible, this is the fat man's keeper.

Here, the Master says, is exhibit "A" of Deity. God does not glower at the back door. He comes down the lane scanning the horizon. And when he sees us, he runs to meet us.

As I look back down the way I've come, I know it's true. There is no counting the number of times I've been given a new beginning. Often I've turned away from him. But never once have I heard God say, "Sorry. You've had your chance."

So we don't need to be ashamed to come back with our broken pledge. Because we are like we are, we may fail. Once. Twice. A dozen times and another dozen. Over and over. Again and again. But because he is like he is, this is the amazing Good News. God is always ready to lift us from our fall and set our feet on the high path again.

＊＊＊＊＊＊＊

PRAYER: Thank you, Lord, for new beginnings.